BREAKING *the* CHAINS

Escaping Abuse, Cults and Finding True Love

LATOYA BRASWELL

CONTENTS

DEDICATION

To all the people who have helped me to crossover and become

The beautiful souls that raised me Mommy, Daddy, Junior, Jermaine and Angie I am better because of each of you.

My circle of strong, poised women, who always lift me up, who have set incredible patterns for me to follow.

My mentors Gerrod and Heather who have kept me pushing spiritually and professionally.

———————

To the loves of my life

Amiee and Ashton, my hearts outside of my body, who are my reasons for being.
Mischa my plus son, you keep me creative.
And finally, Corey, who has allowed me to always be my authentic self, I love you.

PREFACE

As I was finishing this manuscript, I found myself emerging from what felt like a deep pit in my life. The sting of a denied promotion had left me devastated. Rejection had always been a difficult pill for me to swallow, and understanding the reasons behind it was equally challenging. I had dedicated years of tireless work to advance my career as an educator, only to be met with disappointment. During this time, I also faced the heart-wrenching losses of my father and younger brother, leaving an indelible void in my life. The weight of their absence added to the overwhelming emotions I experienced in that moment of rejection. I was at a crossroads, unsure of which path to take.

For six months, I abandoned this very manuscript as I tried to navigate through the complexities of life. I distanced myself from those around me, yearning for solitude and respite from the pain. I had no desire to hear words of encouragement; instead, I contemplated quitting and disconnecting from anything or anyone that could potentially hurt me further. I was consumed by my emotions, and all I asked was for those in my circle to respect my need for space and time to process. But they did not yield. They continued to motivate and uplift me, refusing to let me sink into the depths of despair. They reminded me that rejection can often be a shield, guiding us towards greater things. They urged me to persevere.

It was in that transformative moment that I made a decision. I picked up my pen, determined to bring closure to this body of work. I chose to embrace vulnerability and share my story in the form of a memoir. Within these pages, I hope you will discover great value and apply the lessons I've learned to foster and strengthen your own relationship with God. I hope that spiritual leaders will reflect upon their practices and recognize themselves as servants to God's people, rather than masters to be served. I hope that men, too, will seek healing from past traumas, enabling them to sustain healthy and wholesome relationships. And I hope that women will find their voices, claim their spaces, embrace love, feel their inherent beauty, and live in hopefulness as they learn to think for themselves.

Now, more than ever, I see the profound value in my story, even if it may not be characterized by perfection or prettiness. It is my story—my personal crossover. Within it lies a testament to resilience, personal growth, and the unfathomable strength of the human spirit. As you embark on this journey with me, I invite you to open your heart, embrace your own story, and discover the transformative power that awaits within the pages that follow.

chapter one

A MOVE TO A DIFFERENT CITY

Life will not always give you what you want. Sometimes, you find yourself in a situation you never wished for yourself, a situation you never planned for yourself, and you keep asking yourself, why me? You keep asking yourself if there was anything that you've done wrong for you to deserve all or any of what you are currently experiencing, but no matter how you think about it, you find out that you never did anything wrong; life just happened, and you found yourself in a dark season of your life.

There are so many things we can't control, and one of the things we can't control is one's mindset. We do not have the physical power to control the mindset of people. I do believe we have the power to influence the way the mind perceives various things. Psychology is dedicated to studying the human mind and its functions. It is especially focused on the way the human mind and its function behave in a given context. We dedicate a lot of time and money to try to figure out or understand the mindset of people. It's a complicated, intricate work of art. I don't think we will ever fully comprehend the mind. I know we will never have the power to change one's mindset. That change will have to be intrinsic and the power of the individual.

I wanted the best for myself. I don't think there's anybody out there that wants something bad for themselves or something that is going to put them in a difficult situation. So, I did all I could do to prevent myself from dealing with a difficult situation. We all think we are smart enough not to be gullible, but life has a way of teaching us who we really are through unavoidable difficult situations. When I met Trent. He was not much taller than me, wide build, wore glasses with a nice smile. He generally wore his hair low because he didn't like his curls. I thought his curls were cute. I thought that he was the whole world to me. I was pretty young around then. I wanted to do everything with him; I wanted to spend all my time with him; I was already thinking of the possibility of starting a family with him. That's what love does to you. When you're in a relationship with someone you love, you find yourself thinking about a future with them; you have fantasies of having him permanently in your life. It was all good around that time; I was in love, and I believe that was how it ought to be. I believe love should make you feel free. It should make you feel seen, heard, valued and safe.

I want to say that, at first, it was as if nothing was going to go wrong. I've watched many people put their relationships out there for all to see. Especially on social media. They go on a couple of dates together, meet each other's families, go on a trips together, spend quality time together, and do everything that strengthens their relationship. Sure, there are difficult times that may arise, but those times I believe teach you who you really are. This was what I had wanted, I had a lot of love to give, and I was all out to give it, and I had thought he wanted the same things I wanted. Still, as time went by, I started seeing things that I never thought I was ever going to see from him. If someone had told me around when I met him that this was the person he was, I don't think I would ever have believed them. I didn't know if I would say he pretended to be a nice guy until I fell deeply for him or if I would say that there were red flags, but I didn't get to see them because I was young and probably naive. I believe he thought he was supposed to behave that way because to him that demonstrated his love for me. He had grown up seeing his father mistreat his mother. His mother was mishandled by other men in her life from temporary boyfriends to second and third husbands. He was well aware of the women in his family having relationships outside of their marriage; I now look back at his upbringing being the birthing place of his trauma and his perception of women. His early images of women would shape how he dealt with women and what kinds of relationships he would have with women. I only realized that I was with a totally different person when my worst nightmares started turning into reality.

I used to hear people complaining about how abusive their relationship was, and I had always asked myself, what would make people who are so much in love with each other, suddenly turn abusive towards each other? Or even stay with someone that was abusive for that matter. Like these people loved each other, they spoke with each other, and they decided to start something serious between themselves. So, what would cause all of these things to change. During all these times, they shared wonderful moments together, they built memories together. Still, after all this, these people started acting antagonistically towards each other, it becomes so difficult for both to have a lasting peaceful moment between them just because one of them started acting in ways they were never expected to be acting.

I had seen Trent as the apple of my eye. We had made a lot of promises to each other. We were going to build our family together and have wonderful life. There were a lot of good things we agreed on in the building of our relationship. I had thought that the future was so bright between us that nothing could stop us; all we needed to do was work hard, trust God and remain together. I never knew that remaining together would, at some point, be more than I had bargained for. Trent suddenly became abusive towards me. It started with jealousy and false accusations. It then moved to threats of self-harm. " I will kill myself if you leave me" he would say, then everyone will blame you. I did not want that on my conscious. I tried my best to be the best woman for him, but there was nothing that I ever did that was enough to change his mindset. He always did his best to find fault and made me feel so bad about myself. I was always depressed, and sometimes, I would have to ask myself if I was really in a relationship. I remember we would take pictures, I would pretend to be happy in the picture. One time my close girlfriend whom by the way never cared for Trent said, "you're smiling in this picture but you are not happy". I always thought I could mask my pain with a big smile. He was so insensitive and never cared about my pain; I even had to believe at some point that he was having a lot of delight in seeing me in pain because he was the one going out of his way to cause me these pains. The abuse was verbal; it was physical; it was psychological. Whenever I saw a couple hold hands, smile and laugh at each other, I had to ask myself if it was the same kind of relationship I had with Trent. Everything was so wrong, and I had to ask myself continuously how things could go this wrong. I tried severally to leave, but whenever I tried to leave, I always found myself back with him; it was as if I was like a dot in a circle that wouldn't possibly make any move out of the circle. I saw no growth in my life. I had always been a very ambitious young woman who had a lot of things I wanted to achieve, but being with Trent kind of drained my zeal to get better and do better. His fits of rage and jealousy were unending. "You think you better than me", "You're not", he would say." Whenever I mentioned going back to school to finish my degree. He had stressed me out so much in school that I failed my final and did not receive enough credits to finish my degree. He would come up to the campus and stare in the classroom door to see if I was talking to a guy. I was always stressed out. Trent barely finished high school and was sent to an alternative school for boys when he was around 15 years old because his mother was having trouble with him. I never knew that one's early traumas in life could have this much negative effect on someone until I got into this relationship. At some point, I had to tell myself the truth. One thing about truth is that no matter how you try to suppress it, it will always look for a way to get out; it will always look for a way to make itself known. Yes, I loved Trent, but the truth was that Trent did not love himself. I couldn't possibly have a future with him. Why? Because a future with him would ruin my life or possibly end my life early. He turned my life upside down during those months that I was with him; he turned me into a shadow of myself. I had lost weight, I was losing my hair and a bit of my hearing from all the yelling, arguing and fighting. Eventually those constant blows will affect you in some sort of way. My nerves were bad, and my anxiety was out of control. I was no longer that woman whom I had known myself to be. I had to look for myself, which had been suppressed due to an extended period of abuse. Where was she and could she ever be found?

So, one day, I made the decision and told Trent that it was over and that I didn't want to continue to be with him. Before then, there was this thing I'd come to learn about making decisions. When one wants to make a tough decision that he might end up reversing to favor his adversary, this person must put strong measures in place that would make them never go back and change that very tough decision which they had made. Some people who made tough decisions and then decided to go back on them didn't go back on them because going back on them was the best decision to make; they went back on them because they were pushed to a corner, and they were too weak to continue standing.

I decided that it wasn't just going to be enough to break up with Trent; I would have to create space, and I'll have to stay away from him while I tried to fix my life from what he had shattered it into. So, I decided that I would be leaving the South. The most bothering thing around that time was my parents and some of my relatives, who were very much part of my daily life. My parents were my safety. I always felt loved and validated by my parents. Trent did a good job of trying to keep me away from family and friends. Isolation is a part of an abusive relationship. A good course might be difficult to start, but the product is always worth it. So, I decided I would be moving. I already had somewhere in mind New York City. My biggest challenge around that time was where to stay in New York City. I wasn't the kind of person who enjoys showing up at someone's place and then inconveniencing them. I had always loved my own space. As a result, I have always put others in my shoes to know how to treat them. I never forgot my struggles. I keep them in my mind as I go through life. I think of how I felt during the lowest points in my life and how I can help someone that may be in my shoes. But in this case, I didn't have any option. I didn't have a house in NEW YORK CITY; I was going to go there to start my life afresh, to pick my life up and look for what to do with it. I didn't want to stay with just anybody; a family member would be somewhat better, even though I wouldn't stay there for too long. So, my sister was staying in NEW YORK CITY around that time. I agreed to stay with her; I never planned to stay for long at her place, and there were reasons for this.

At this point in my life, I had learned to prioritize prayers. I never saw the importance of prayers until I started seeing them working wonders. I was from a religious family. My mother served as an associate pastor in her church. My parents did their best to raise us up in church and to teach us to pray, so I was always praying and talking to God about whatever move I wanted to make. I was taught to acknowledge God in all my ways and He will direct my path. I had this feeling that relocating to NEW YORK CITY was a good decision. Although it was a new environment for me as an adult and I was going under unique circumstances. I knew I had to get there, I had to leave the South if I wanted to save my life. I planned to get there, get a good job, save some money, and then get my apartment. I didn't want to be dependent on anyone, so I was out to work hard and get things done.

I missed my parents a lot when I went to NEW YORK CITY, I knew I would be returning soon to see them, but that was going to take a long while before I would return to the South to see my parents; in fact, the truth was that they were the only reasons I would be returning to the South anytime soon. Around when I eventually left for NEW YORK CITY, I was twenty-one. I was full of life but was so down casted by the pains and damages that I had gone through in my previous relationship. At just twenty-one, I already had experienced trauma, endured abuse, operated under a clouded mindset but still had willingness to crossover to a better side of life.

When I got to NEW YORK CITY I had about three outfits and one pair of shoes. Trent had destroyed all my clothes when I told him I was leaving him. Once I arrived one of the first things, I did was to get a job. I already had some money saved $120 to be exact. But I had to get a job so I wouldn't end up getting broke within a short time and having to ask Trent for help or return down south. I searched for a job, and within a short period, I was employed. I was starting a new life, and even without being told, I already knew within myself that I had to work hard, I hard to earn a lot of money, and not just earn a lot of money but also learn to save the money I would be making, if I wanted to do something with my life.

chapter two

FRUITLESS FIRST TRIAL

've come to learn something about life. Sometimes, when you're desperately looking for something. When you desire something so badly, you might not get that thing around that time. This is one irony of life that most of us might not be ready to accept yet. After I got to New York City, I started working and earning money. I gradually adapted to life there. So, at some point, I decided that it was time for me to look for somewhere I would stay, somewhere I would have some of my own space. I was staying with my sister and her friend then, but I knew it was the right time for me to move. She had done more than enough for me by letting me stay in her house. So, there was this family friend I was talking to, and he told me that this pastor was interested in subletting their apartment. Immediately when I heard that the person who wanted to sublet their apartment was a pastor; I told myself that this would be good for me. In a society filled with many things that want to derail you from the things of God, a society filled with a lot of distractions, having someone who is responsible for leading people in the right direction toward God interested in subletting her apartment to me made me feel that this was definitely God granting me favor again.

So, I thought about how best to meet this pastor. She was a busy pastor with many things going on for her. So, I had to think of how best to meet her without inconveniencing her. I also must look for a way that would be somewhat easier for me. As I was thinking about meeting this pastor, the only reasonable way was to go to her church and meet her after the service. This is usually the best time to speak with or meet the pastor after the service on Sunday; Although the conversations that go on around this time are always brief, at least they're something. Some people usually get to book an appointment to speak with the pastor later just from those brief conversations. So, I was going to meet the pastor in person and discuss the apartment; after our discussion, I would know the next step to take.

So, I was briefed by my family friend who told me about this pastor about the times I could go to the church and find her. The perfect time to meet her was during the Wednesday night prayer service. I was given the church's location since I had never been to the church before. I was trying my best to get to the church earlier so that I would at least be a part of what would be happening during the night, but before I could get there, the prayer was already going on. As I approached the storefront church, I started hearing the strong sound of prayer. It reminded of my childhood church in Bryds, South Carolina. These people were seriously praying to God. They meant business as they were very focused on the prayers they had gathered for. They were there as intercessors. Praying and standing in the gap for others was their mission. There was no-one at the front of the church as I approached, so I decided to walk inside. There was strong praying going on from the pulpit; the sound was everywhere; it was the sound of someone that had migrated from the realm of the physical to the realm of the spirit. I then walked into the church; I was so curious to see who was praying with such a powerful resonance, you could feel the impact of the prayer once you're within the vicinity, and I wouldn't deny the fact that I was moved by the prayers that were going on and I felt the presence of God in that moment. When I walked in at first, I couldn't see anyone at the pulpit, and I must have been looking at the wrong side. So, I got closer to the pulpit, and this was when I saw her. She was lying and prostrating on the floor of the pulpit while she was praying; I was close enough to notice tears streaming down her face as she prayed. I was moved by what I had just seen.

I wouldn't deny that I was so in awe that one could be so connected in prayer that it was as if only her and God was in the room. For one to have prayed to this length, one must have been so connected spiritually. You don't get that far in prayers when you allow your mind to wallow about many things. Sometimes we want to pray, and we find out that many things that had been bothering us continue to stream into our hearts. These things come in, and they make us continue praying and not be fully focused on the prayers which we're saying. These things we are facing take our focus from connecting spiritually to God as we pray. We pray the problem and not the promise. I've noticed that most times, the things that come into our mind to distract our prayers are always events that had happened in the past or the events or schedules which we had the intention of executing in the future, probably after our prayers. They come into our thoughts, we think through them, and they end up distracting our prayers. When one is praying, and this person is this distracted, you notice that the spirit doesn't flow; that the frequency of prayer is restricted. it just looks as if they're saying some words to pass the time. But this woman was praying; she was interceding, she was traveling in prayer. I knew right then that God was in the room, and I knew right then that this was the right time for me to render my supplication before God. Around that time, I had a lot of problems in my life, I had a lot of things that were bothering me, but one of them was bothering me so much around that time, and this was the fact that I was yet to have my own place to stay. It was a lot going on in the house I was living in, and I just wanted to be out of there. There is a peace that comes with having your place; there is this freedom that comes with having your place; I was yet to have either of these, so I was still feeling very much not settled in New York City. I believed that once I was able to find my own place, once I was able to find my own space, I would be able to say "yes, I am making progress towards getting my life together and I can make it without Trent.

I closed my eyes and joined in the prayer service. I had to connect to the prayer that was going on. My mind was so bothered by my problems. I had to push hard in order to align myself with the prayers going on. I prayed to God and told Him that I needed to get my own place; I needed to fix my life. I knew that my life was thrown into total shambles before I made my way to NEW YORK CITY, and before I made my move to NEW YORK CITY, I told

God that I wanted him to fix my life by the time I got to NEW YORK CITY. So, I told God that I was now in NEW YORK CITY, and I acknowledged all that he had done for me but there were still some ways I needed to be made. I need something new in my life. Isaiah 43:19 " Behold I will do a new thing, now it shall spring forth, shall you not know it ? I will even make a way in the wilderness and rivers in the desert. The prayers lasted long enough to allow me to pour out my heart to God. I reminded Him what I went through in my previous relationship and how important it was for me to get my apartment so that I would be better than what my previous relationship had subjected me to; the bible says that those who trust in the lord will be experiencing a lifting up when others would be saying that there is a casting down in their lives. I prayed to my Father in heaven without minding who was seeing or who was hearing. I was there until the prayer service was over. I felt even more confident my prayers were heard and going to be answered. When you cast your burden to the Lord, He will help you carry them and ease the burden. Most of the problems we have with whatever we see as our problems are not just the fact that they're our problems. It is the very fact that they bother us, inconvenience us, and take our peace of mind from us, so I was somewhat at peace even though I didn't know what the conversation with the pastor was going to turn out to be. Of course, she could turn me down, it was a possibility, and at this point, my mind was prepared to take whatever for an answer. That's what happens when you're able to build confidence. When you're able to build confidence, even amid rejection, you'll be able to find success.

So, I stayed there until the prayer service was over. After the prayer service was over, I was eager to see what would happen next. This point was very important to me because it would help me conclude how to make my moves on seeing her. I was there for the first time, I had never been there before, so I didn't know what would be next or what she would do next after the prayer service. I was watching to get every detail of what was happening. As I was watching, I saw some women take her into a small office. Around this point, I didn't know why she was taken into this small office, I had thought that perhaps it was like they were going there to have some conversation, but I later found out that the main reason for going into the small office was for her to change her clothes. That was pretty much understandable with the style of prayer I had watched her pray; she was soaked in her own perspiration, her hair was frazzled, her eyes where red behind her glasses she wore on her face from crying. She appeared as though she had been in a battle and was determined not to be defeated. I would also want to change if I were in her shoes. When she went into the small office, I figured out that the prayer session was over since some of the people around were already making their way home. It wasn't time for me to go home since I had a business that had brought me to the church; the prayer session that I happened to have taken part in was just like a bonus. I thought about the right place to wait for her. I knew that there were places where I could wait, and I might end up not having to see her and she could see me before she left to return home so I could at least talk with her. So, I waited at the back of the church. The spot was reasonable enough because once she came out of the small office, there was no way we wouldn't end up meeting each other with me staying there. She didn't come out quickly enough, but I continued to wait as I was so determined that no matter what, I would be meeting and talking to her that night.

It took a while, but she eventually came out, and I was relieved to see her. It was as if she knew I was waiting for her, so she just walked towards me. This made things easier for me. I introduced myself to her, and she smiled at me without giving me any special recognition regarding her knowing about the apartment. I was told by my family friend that he had told her about me, so I was hoping that once I introduced myself, we would quickly start our conversation about why I wanted to see her. She introduced herself as Pastor Ruth. I already knew that was her name, so it didn't sound new to me, but I had to play along with the smile on my face. So, I was thinking about how to start the conversation. Since Pastor Ruth had already been briefed about me, I was expecting that she would say that she was told about me and that she was informed that I would be coming to see her because of the apartment. I told myself that once she said this, I would go on into the conversation. When you're having a conversation with someone, what they say determines what your response is going to be to them. When they say something, you should not give a response that doesn't correspond with what they said. So, I was going to say what was on my mind based on how she would react to my presence, but she never spoke about the apartment. It made me question if she knew that I was there for the apartment.

"I'm so glad you are here." Pastor Ruth said to me. "Thank you, pastor; I must confess that the prayer service was so edifying." I responded. "It had always been like this. Once the prayers are going on, the Holy Spirit moves around; He searches our hearts, identifies our problems, and helps us overcome them by solving them for us. But there is something very important that a lot of us don't know. Most times, those things which we identify as problems that are so pressing to us are, in fact, not seen as a problem to God. In fact, God sees it as an opportunity to draw us closer to him. Therefore, we should change our perspective on problems and view them as a bridge to keep us connected to God and God connected to us. Sometimes, these things are just like nothing before God. Whenever God wants to visit us at the point of our problems, He searches for our needs, those needs which are so pressing to us; He settles them for us. Now, most times, this need that God had solved for us might not look like the most pressing need for us in our sight. We might be considering another need as more important, but God decided to do that one, which we probably didn't consider too pressing. This is God in action. Th bible says that the wisdom of man is like foolishness unto God. Some of those needs that God settles for us often open the way to solving all other needs in our lives. It opens the door also to solve all those things we want for ourselves in our lives. I don't think there is anyone in the world that have no problems; the question then becomes do they see their problems as a bridge to the problem solver. whenever a prayer has been said, people always have one or two things which they would want to pray about, but God is always the one to decide on the prayers that he would bring its answers to manifestation. God answers all prayers but brings some into manifestation quicker than others. That's why the word of God teaches us to wait on the Lord and be of good cheer and he will strengthen your heart, so there is a benefit in waiting on God" Pastor Ruth explained. It sounded like a sermon to me. I wouldn't say that I didn't understand all that she had just said; I also wouldn't say that she wasn't right in what she had said. Her words probably showed that she got an idea of what I've been through, and what I wanted, but she never got to speak about it directly, and this made it difficult for me to jump into the conversation with why I had decided to come to the church. "Your words are so deep and true." I replied to the pastor. "I would like to invite you to be here Sunday, we are having a special service, and in this service, I would be elevated to the office of an Apostle, the highest office in the church." Pastor Ruth demanded, she was calm in her demand, but I felt like this demand was something she didn't want me to refuse or something she pressed on me because she knew I would never turn it down. "Wow, it's so great to know that you will be elevated soon. Congratulations.' I said to her. "I would like you to be there to witness me take my new office as an Apostle in the lord's church." Pastor Ruth said to me. "Sure, I will be there." I responded. I never knew a woman Apostle before; in fact, I had never met any Apostles. I only read about Apostles in the bible. I was completely shocked. I knew I had to be there to witness this service. I needed something from her, so there was no way I could turn down the first request that she was making from me. I've always heard people say that the first impression that people make with people they're just meeting for the first time matters a lot. When you make a good first impression with someone, you're just meeting for the first time, it goes a long way to determining what your relationship is going to be with this person onwards. Some people start building hate for people they never knew before, people they had never had anything in common with before, and people that were never part of their lives before, mainly because of the first impression they had with these people. I've heard about people who went for a job interview and just from how they conducted themselves, they found out from the person that was going to interview them that they were not hired for the job, like these people didn't like them, and through their actions, made them realize that they were never going to offer them the job. So, I wanted to create a good first impression with Ruth; I didn't want to create an impression that I was turning down her request that I should show up to the church when she was going to be made an apostle.

After I had assured Pastor Ruth that I would be in the church when she would be made an apostle, I suddenly noticed from her body language that she was done with talking to me, or should I say she was done with our conversation. I've been around people long enough to know when they didn't want a conversation to continue. In my experience, I didn't think it was nice to try to continue a conversation with someone after you've noticed that they weren't comfortable with continuing that conversation with you. If you continue to force the conversation with them, you'll end up not getting anything close to the result that you're looking for. Before I could think about what to say to get more of pastor Ruth's attention, she patted my shoulder and started walking away." God bless you, see you Sunday" she said. It was so difficult having a lengthy conversation with her; it wasn't going to be possible since she just wanted to pass along some specific information and probably didn't want to listen to anything else I had to say, after I agreed to come to her elevation service. I was meeting her for the first time; I didn't know much about her personality; not like I didn't know who she was or what she was doing; I didn't know the kind of person she was around that time. As she walked away, I stood watching her; I felt like I was losing my first chance to have a conversation about the apartment, which was the main reason why I had shown up to the church. It was my first chance, but I watched it slip away from me, and I knew that it wasn't my fault. At that time, I discovered that if you're looking for something in the hands of someone more comfortable than you, there would most likely be a particular kind of relationship between the both of you; it will always be a relationship where those people whom you're trying to get something from will always take the lead while you follow. It can be a pivotal point in your life when you are trying to get something from them that is so important to you. They have the ability in that moment to position you for purpose or position for pauperism. So, you set your intentions on yielding to this person beyond your limits to get the very things from them that will help change your life. As for them, it might look as if they got nothing to gain from you, and because of this reason, they might always act as if they have no real use for you, but I got to find out later that this is not entirely true. I don't think there is anybody out there that is not important; everyone has a good use which they could be put into. Some of these people that happen to be the ones in control of this kind of relationship which I'm talking about, don't get to know how much those people that are under their control are to them until they end up becoming so much dependent on them. If this relationship continues, they will continue to use these people under their control to the very point that they'll exploit them beyond measures and say it was in the name of God.

As I watched the pastor leave, I wasn't disappointed that I would be coming to the church to witness her elevation to the office of an apostle. I was disappointed that I met her, but I couldn't even have that very conversation that brought me there.

chapter three

WORKING WITH DISAPPOINTMENT

After Pastor Ruth left the church, she got into her car that was waiting outside, and they drove her home. I then walked out of the church and started heading home. I would say that the disappointment I had became more pronounced on me after I started going home. Throughout the trip home, I felt bothered by the fact that I was at the mercy of someone. I was looking for a comfortable place to stay at very little cost because of how things were with me around that time; this was why I had to be subjected to the situation I found myself in.

I got home to my sister's place. I confined myself to solitude as I thought about my conversation with Pastor Ruth. It wasn't a bad conversation, but I was so bothered that at some point, I had begun thinking that maybe she was not told that I was coming, or maybe the family friend didn't tell her explicitly that I was coming. I had to pick up my phone and call this family friend. I had told this family friend earlier that I was going to see Pastor Ruth that day, so this family friend was eager to know the outcome of our meeting. She asked me immediately after she picked up my call about how the meeting with Pastor Ruth went. I told him what our conversation was like. He had asked me if that was all, and I told him yes, that I was even going to ask him if she spoke with pastor Ruth. My family friend told me that he told her about me and that he was sure that pastor Ruth was expecting me. So, I was kind of not understanding what was happening. If this pastor wanted to have me to have her apartment, she should have at least told me that she was informed that I would be coming to see her. This made me feel even worse about my situation. Still, I wasn't going to give up, I was the one looking to get something from her, and I already gave my word that I was going to be present on the day that she would be elevated to the office of an apostle.

Later in the night, my sister came around and asked me about my visit to the church to see Pastor Ruth; I had been reluctant to tell her anything about it because she had been around her roommate. So, I told her what happened; she told me that there was no way I would expect everything to go as quickly as I had wanted it to go. It was going to take time, and if the Pastor had acted as if she didn't know why I had come to the church, she wasn't going to blame her; maybe she was trying to know if I was the kind of person she could have in her apartment. Some people would not want to take just anyone into their homes because of their own personal reasons. Some people could come into someone's house and start constituting a nuisance to them. Even though I didn't quite agree with my sister, I didn't argue about it. Sunday was a few days away, so it wouldn't do much harm if I had to wait until Sunday.

I could remember waking very early on Sunday. My mom had called me very early that morning to know how I was doing; I had told her that I was holding on. I didn't tell her that I was trying to get an apartment because, at that time, I wasn't even sure what would be the outcome of seeing Pastor Ruth. The first time I had gone to the church, I was hoping that by the time I would be returning to my sister's place, I would have had a clear lead on what I was going to be doing next, pertaining to having my own space, but things didn't turn the way that I had expected.

I finished up with some of the stuff I had scheduled to do that morning before I started getting ready for church. My sister and her roommate didn't have plans to leave the house that morning, so I just left them and went to the church. As I approached the church, I heard a lot of singing. I wanted to be in the church with the first people that would be showing up. I wanted to sit in the front so that she could see that I was there. I wanted her to see that she could trust me at my word. I hoped that this would in some way translate that I was a good, trustworthy young woman that would take care of her apartment. I wanted to sit in the front, but the front was reserved for clergy. I walked into the church; the church was scarcely filled, so I figured out that maybe they didn't have a lot of people attending or maybe I was too early compared to those that were yet to show up in the church. It was my second time in the church; I didn't know much about how the services were conducted. Normally, when I find myself at a place like this, I always prefer to look for a place where I wouldn't be discovered easily and just stay there while I observe whatever was going on there. But this time, there was no way I would sit at a spot where no-one would see me. A part of me felt like I was there to impress Pastor Ruth. I wouldn't say I wasn't there because I wanted to be in the house of God. I've always been a spiritual woman, even though I wasn't too sure about where I was at in my walk with God. I loved God but didn't understand why I was going through all these adversities. I often questioned what I did to deserve this. So, I had my reservations about even attending this church with this Pastor that has not yet mentioned anything about the intent for the encounter.

The thing was that I never planned to be there that Sunday. If my visit to the church the previous day went successfully, I might not have shown up in the church that Sunday, unless Pastor Ruth had asked for it. So, I wanted Pastor Ruth to know that I was in the church and that I was in the church earlier enough to witness everything that was happening in the church during her elevation to the office of an Apostle. There was a lot of singing, praising, and preaching going on. More people started to arrive in priestly garments there was a section dedicated for family. There wasn't a lot of family members. For a moment, I forgot why I was there. When the spirit is moving and you commit yourself to be in the flow of what is happening that is bigger than you, you find yourself flowing in the move. I must admit that was the best part of the service really experiencing the presence of God.

After an extended moment of singing, clapping, and dancing, it was time for us to listen to the sermon. I had expected that pastor Ruth would be the one to give the sermon that day, but there were other Apostles and Bishops seated there. These were leaders that had been in the field longer than her; you could easily conclude from their ages and how they were conducting themselves. So, while we were all seated with our eyes on the pulpit, one of the Apostles stood up then walked to the pulpit. He said this is the Lords doing and it is marvelous in his sight. I welcome you to the consecration and affirmation service of Apostle Ruth. We pray that God's anointing would be in this service. The sermon he preached was "You need Judas" In the message he talked about Judas getting you to your destiny. Judas will push you into what God has chosen for you. Don't be afraid of Judas. No Judas no fulfillment of your purpose. Judas was a part of Jesus's purpose. As he ministered, I began to think about the Judas in my life and realize that my Judas is helping me to get to my purpose.

After the sermon, there were a lot of things that went on, and then the main occasion of the day. Pastor Ruth was then elevated to the office of an Apostle, they laid hands on her, washed her feet, dressed her in priestly garments. She vowed to honor the sacrate office of the Apostle. After they had her to turn and face the congregation as they presented her for the first time as an Apostle. Everyone in the church felt happy for her. They acknowledged the fact that her elevation was long due. I wasn't going to this church before, so I just stayed there and listened to them say all they were saying about her and how God had been using her mightily. The church seemed to be in a great spirit that day. The service lasted for a very long time, and I started wondering how her life was going to be now that she was an Apostle. At some point we would have the conversation about the apartment, but it surely was not going to be that day.

I waited patiently for the church to be over for the day. I kept telling myself that no matter what, I wouldn't leave until I finally got to speak with Pastor Ruth. The service finally ended, and it felt like a lot of loads had been taken off my head. After the church ended for the day, I waited at a spot where I knew Pastor Ruth could see me. I saw her looking at me at one point from her seat with other pastors. Other pastors came around from other churches to witness her elevation. So, they were having some conversation with her while I waited. When I caught her looking at me, she waved at me to indicate that she knew that I was there. I was relieved that she had seen that I was there and waiting for her. This meant that whatever she would be doing, she would try and be somewhat quick so that we would meet and have a conversation about the apartment.

The conversation that Ruth was having with these pastors took a long time. I didn't know what they were talking about to have taken that long. They were all in the field of leading the church, and there was no way they wouldn't be interacting from time to time. I stayed for like twenty minutes after the service had ended, a lot of people should have gone home, but there were still some people hanging around in the church and within the church premises. I couldn't understand why these people were sticking around. I was wondering if there was another church activity that should be held probably about an hour later. Pastor Ruth soon finished her conversation with the pastors that were with her. She then moved away from where she was sitting with them at the pulpit and then came down to the area meant for the congregation; I was now thinking in my mind that maybe she was coming to me, perhaps she knew I had been waiting, and I even came around to the church as I had promised I was going to do, so, perhaps she wanted us to be done with the conversation so that I would get on my way home. I was expectant as relief was gradually taking over me. Suddenly, I saw something which I was never expecting to happen. It was like suspense in a movie unfolding in a way the viewer had never expected. Most of the congregation that had stayed behind quickly met Pastor Ruth. She was accosted just as she stepped down from the pulpit and was still looking around for the next thing to do. These people in her congregation wanted to congratulate her on her elevation. Some wanted to congratulate her and then speak with her about certain things that had been happening in their lives. I was left dumbfounded after I realized that most of those that had waited after the service was over were waiting to meet Pastor Ruth. She probably knew they were waiting for her, and that was why she got out from the pulpit to allow them to meet with her and tell her whatever they had in mind to tell her.

I just sat there watching what was happening; I don't think there was any right word that would be able to describe the mood which I found myself in around that time. How quickly the hope I had bought got crushed kind of surprised me. All these people wanted to speak with one person, and I was seated and waiting for this person. I felt some traces of frustration building inside of me. Sometimes you try to see if you could suppress it or make it disappear, but we're all humans, and we sometimes end up feeling that very way we had tried our best not to feel.

I could see that, at this point that Ruth was busy; there was no way she would send all of these people away just because she wanted to see me. These people were having conversations with her while she was standing. Whatever they were saying to her was as brief as possible, and she was giving them a brief response that was brief enough not to take too much of her time since many of her church members wanted to speak with her.

I waited for close to an hour; then I started seeing the pastors seated at the pulpit getting up. It was obvious that these people were going to leave the premises. I told myself that I had no use for them around that time. The sermon given by one of them was so inspiring, it was a beautiful sermon, but at that point, I wasn't thinking about the sermon; I was thinking about my conversation with Ruth. If she could finish up with these people, then we could talk. I kept trying to console myself by telling myself that it was almost my time to speak to her, but then, suddenly. One of the pastors walked up to her a whispered into her ear. After this pastor whispered into Ruth's ear, she told the people still standing to speak to her that she had somewhere she must go to with the pastors waiting for her. She then directed the members to meet her around Tuesday because she would be around in the church to speak with them in her office. Ruth was a very successful businesswoman; even though she was a Pastor doing her best to give the best to her work as a Pastor, she was serious about her finances, credit and investments.

''As I was still seated and watching Pastor Ruth, hoping that she would look at the side where I was seated and maybe ask me to come or give me a clue of what I was going to do. She didn't do anything to show that she knew I had been waiting. After talking to some of the people that had been waiting to speak to her, Ruth quickly started walking out of the church together with those pastors that had been around her. I remained seated and watched her while she walked to the exit door of the church. Ruth left the church, and quickly got into her car and drove off with those pastors that had come for her elevation service to the office an Apostle.

After Ruth left, I felt so bad about myself. It was so bad to accept the reality that I had been in the church for the second time and had not had any productive conversation with Ruth. The situation that played out before me looked as if I wasn't going to blame her completely for how things turned around, but if I didn't blame her, who was I going to blame? Was I going to blame myself? I did what she asked me to do; she had asked me to show up to the church that day, I did as I had said I was going to do, but she ended up getting me disappointed again for the second time. She had people who were following her around, about two different people. I felt these people were her assistants in the church. If she wanted to pass a message across to me, like at least ask me to come another day, and appeal to me not to be mad at what had happened, she would have just given one of her ministers a note to give to me, and this would make me feel seen. At this point, I felt as if I wasn't seen. I felt as if I was constituting a nuisance. At that moment, I felt like just giving up on the apartment. I stood up from where I was seated and walked out of the church. After Ruth left the church, the number of people that had gathered to see her diminished as some of them started making their way home.

I walked quietly and left the church premises without speaking to anyone. It was as if I was someone with no single value. At some point, I started wondering how it would be to live in an apartment owned by Ruth. How could she do this to me? I told myself that I didn't deserve this. I concluded within myself that I was going to get an alternative to Pastor Ruth. I didn't want to go back to her again. I was noy getting any closer to my prayer request by following her up with her request and still not even having a conversation about my need. So, when I got home, my mind was already settled that there was nothing I would be doing anywhere close to Ruth's church again.

I was laying on the sofa around 3:30 PM; I'd been mad throughout the whole day that I decided to stay in solitude. I eventually dozed off to sleep while lying on the sofa. This was when I heard my phone ringing. I was sleepy around that time, so I just picked up the phone and positioned it to my ear without looking at the screen to know who it was that was calling my phone. Then I heard a voice which I couldn't recognize talk from the other end. "How have you been?" She asked me. "I'm fine," I responded while I tried to see if there was any way I could identify the voice that was talking to me from the other end. "The Lord blessed us mightily today; I believe you experienced the presence of God." The voice from the other end said. Immediately I heard her talk about today's service; I sat on the sofa as I could now recognize whom I was talking to. It was Pastor Ruth. I was particularly surprised that she got my number. My family friend that had connected us never told me she gave Ruth my number unless, of course, Ruth called her to request my number after she realized that I wasn't happy over how I couldn't talk to her that day despite how long I waited to speak to her.

"Sure. I was touched right from when the songs were going on to the sermon. Congratulations, by the way, on your elevation." I said to her over the phone. "Thank you. I've gotten a lot of that today; God is good." Ruth said on the phone. I was so busy today I couldn't attend to all those that wanted to see me today. Can you come around on Tuesday?" Ruth asked me. "Tuesday?" I responded without knowing what would happen on Tuesday. "Yeah, we'll be having our counseling session from 9:00 AM to 2:00 PM; if you can come around, then you could meet me in my office at the church," Ruth said to me. "Okay, that would be great," I responded, even though I knew that I was at work around the time that she wanted to meet me in her office. The fact that she called me on the phone kind of changed my mood and the way I had felt since I left the church, but she could have just allowed us to have the conversation over the phone. I didn't understand why it was taking this long, but I concluded that I would go and see her because she called me.

After my phone conversation with Pastor Ruth, I was very curious as to how she got my number. I perceived she got my number from my family friend, but I was not 100% sure. So, I called my family friend, and we got talking. He asked me about my visit to the church that day and that he was yet to call pastor Ruth and congratulate her on her elevation. Now, the conversation was getting interesting as I heard my family friend say that he was yet to place a call to Pastor Ruth. Honestly, I had thought that Pastor Ruth had called my family friend earlier that day and had asked him to give her my number, but this didn't seem to be the case. "I thought you already spoke to her today," I said in slight confusion. "No, I didn't. Why do you think I spoke to her today?" My family friend asked. "She called me today. I finished speaking with her before I decided to give you a call. I was surprised she called, so I thought that maybe you gave her the number, which was why she decided to call me. "Well, I gave her your number, but it's been a while since I gave her it. I gave her your number the first day I spoke to her about you." My family friend explained. I didn't know how to react to the fact that the Pastor had my number all this time, and she only thought about calling me after she figured out, I wasn't happy over how things went at the church that day.

After my conversation with my family relative, I got up and headed to the kitchen to get myself something to eat while I thought about how I would go to the church by Tuesday. The main issue was my job. I was new to this job, and abandoning my work just like that and going to see Pastor Ruth was a decision I would look have to make without ending up getting myself into trouble at my place of work. I had to figure out how to go about it.

In the early hours of Monday morning, I was sleeping on the sofa when I noticed that my phone was ringing. The time was around 1:15 AM. I didn't know who would be calling around this time. I looked at the screen of the phone to know who it was that was calling me, the number was a strange number. I picked it up because I believed that whoever was calling me around that time must have something important that they were trying to talk to me about.

"Hello, babe." I heard a familiar voice from the other end say to me. It was the voice of a drunk man. I had to take the phone off my ear and look at the screen again to ensure I didn't have the number saved on my phone. I then put the phone back to my ear. I already knew that Trent was the one talking from the other end. He was drunk, as always. I remained quiet while I had the phone positioned to my ear. "I know you're there; I know that you're in New York City. Did you think you can run away from me?" Trent asked he must be trying to be calm, but I could smell threats in his voice. "You can't run away from me, babe. You know I love you, and I can't just let you stay away from me. No other nigga has the right to have you; you belong to me, and I know you know that." Trent said. I could see that he still had his entitlement mentality eating up on him. He had never thought I would ever be able to walk out of his life. I've made several efforts in the past and ended up failing, but this time, I meant every bit of it when I said it was over. I had told him that I was done with him, but I didn't tell him that I was going to New York City. He was a stalker that could abandon everything he was doing to talk to someone for a whole week. I was done with that life; with someone ruining and trying to destroy my life; right now, I had taken back my life, and I wanted to make something meaningful out of it.

''Why are you not talking? I know you're listening to me; you should say something.'' Trent said while he waited very briefly for me to respond. ''Say something, you black bitch!'' Trent yelled. "You up there with another nigga and I know it". This was who he was; whatever he couldn't get from me out of my freewill, he'll always try to get it by force. I didn't know how I stayed all these years with this person. It was as if a scale had fallen off my eyes; I was never ready to use my hands to put that scale back onto my eyes just to pretend that I didn't see, hear or feel what I was experiencing in that moment. Immediately he yelled at me; "Tell your mother to buy you a white dress cause that's what they are going to bury you in". I had to hang up the phone. I didn't know how he was able to find out that I was in New York City, but with the kind of friends I had down south, there was no way he wasn't going to know. Now, I see things somewhat differently from how I used to see things in the past. If you want to record a lot of growth in your life, sometimes you must add by subtraction. We don't always like the breakup or when people must be removed out of our lives. But I have learned that God allows removal in order to make room. Addition by subtraction means some things must be taken away for the beneficial thing to be added. Your surroundings can impact your growth or what is perceived as growth. The bible speaks of a certain man having a fig tree in his vineyard, he comes seeking fruit and finds none. He informs the vinedresser that for years he has been coming seeking fruit from this tree but has found none. He says CUT IT DOWN. The cutting down can represent subtraction. If a relationship is not being fruitful, then cut it down. We often misinterpret leaves as growth but if a tree is purposed to bear fruit but does not then that tree has missed its purpose cut it down. And that was what my relationship was a "fruitless tree" that had to be cut down.

It was Tuesday morning. I had to wake up early and get to work earlier than I had always. I planned to do as much as possible for the day on time; then I would plead for a co-worker to cover my shift while I went to see Pastor Ruth. I was willing to do a double shift for my co-worker, in order to secure the early shift off. My regular schedule was from 6am-2pm the double would allow me to do work form 6am-10pm therefore I could be off that morning.

So, I did my double shift, it was a long day, I was tired, I was nervous. I really didn't know if I was coming or going. I was always looking over my shoulder not knowing when Trent would appear. I had no one to confide in, when you are in these kinds of situations everyone and I mean everyone has a opinion about what they would do if they were you. I used to be one of the people with an opinion about everything, until I became the victim. Everything I said I would never do; I did. What I said I wouldn't tolerate, I did. So, during this time I had to taste my own words and trust me they were not sweet.

By 11:00 AM, I was already on a bus heading towards the church. It wasn't much of a ride. I stayed on the bus for like ten minutes before I alighted and walked for a few minutes to get to the church. By the time I got to the church, it was 11:45 AM. I believed that the only reason I had taken a bit to get to the church was because I had to stand a bit longer, waiting for the bus that would convey me towards the direction where the church was located.

I was on the church premises, and I could see some people around the church, but it was not many. Most of them were waiting to speak to Pastor Ruth. So, without wasting any time, I went and joined the queue. I noticed that the queue was taking too long; those that were going into Ruth's office were taking longer to come out of the office; I was wondering how long I was going to wait before it was going to get my turn. The whole thing was becoming uncomfortable. So, while waiting, I decided to use my time properly. I decided that I would have a moment of prayer, and after that, I would return and then stay in the queue again; maybe around then, it would be almost my turn to see Pastor Ruth. It sounded like a good idea. I had to tell those behind them in the queue that I was going to have a brief prayer and then return to join the queue; they assured me that my position would be secured as long as I wouldn't take too long to return to the queue. So, I left immediately.

I went to the front seat in the church and knelt. The environment was so quiet. Even those waiting to meet Pastor Ruth weren't even heard from where I was kneeling. This place was so good for prayers. One could pray for hours without anyone walking up to them to distract them. So, I started praying. I talked to God about my life. I told Him that I had just started my life afresh with no clear path to where my life was heading. I wanted Him to be my guide; I wanted Him to direct me along the right path. One of the worst mistakes I made in the past was not waiting on God. I believed at the time that getting married and doing what the church called "right" was the way to go. "You don't want to live in sin". To me that meant: you don't want to be having premarital sex". To be honest I didn't want to, my desire was to be married. So, I rushed into a relationship that could have been to my demise. I wondered was I living in sin, because nothing about this situation reflected "God" or anything that was right". I didn't want anyone to be right about me being too young. I didn't want to be a failure.

So, I told God that I wanted him to help me meet the right people, people who would bring positivity into my life, people who wouldn't turn around and intentionally hurt me. I didn't want to do whatever I wanted to do anymore. I wanted God to order my steps. I wanted God to influence my mindset and my decisions. I moved to NEW YORK CITY with a lot of dreams. These dreams had always been with me but had been dormant without me making enough effort towards actualizing them. I thought at times it was too late. I told God I wanted Him to help me to recover the lost time. Joel 2:25 says "I will repay you for the years the locusts have eaten". I was ready for the repayment. I wanted God to activate those dreams in NEW YORK CITY. I told Him that I wasn't expecting things to be easy for me. I knew things would be difficult, but no matter what, I was ready to remain standing if He would lead and direct me.

I didn't want to go about doing things on my own anymore; I needed his direction and to follow his voice in every area of my life. "Lord, I surrender" I cried out. Then I spoke to God about the apartment. I wanted everything to go smoothly; I told Him that if it was His will make everything work out smoothly; make my conversation with Pastor Ruth such that it would turn around in my favor. After that, I prayed for my parents. My mom had told me that morning that she was not feeling her best, so I had to pray for her to recover quickly. I always prayed for my mother. It was my mother that instilled prayer in me and taught me how to pray. I was so into the prayer that I didn't know that time was going so quickly, but not as quickly as to say I spent too much time while praying. After I was done praying, I looked at my wristwatch; it was 12:55 PM. I had prayed for close to forty minutes. I have never prayed so long before. It did not feel long because I was experiencing a lifting in my spirit. I learned in that moment that prayer will elevate you to another level of peace right amid your storm. The more you pray the closer you will get to a peaceful place in your mindset. I knew that I had shared my heart with God. I felt so confident that God had heard my heart and it was no way he was not going to work things out for me.

I then got up from where I was kneeling and then headed back to join the queue. I was surprised that when I got to the place where those people seated in the queue were, I didn't find anyone there. I was confused as the thought that Pastor Ruth might have attended to all of them came to my head. I thought about the possibility that she might have attended to all of them, but it didn't make sense at all. It was taking around ten to fifteen minutes to attend to just one person; there was no way she could have attended to everybody seated there and waiting to see her within forty minutes. I had to figure out another reason that was good enough for those seated and waiting to be attended to by Pastor Ruth to have left and possibly gone home. Then my eyes went towards Ruth's office. There was a passage leading to her office door. This passage had a door always opened whenever Pastor Ruth was around. I noticed that this door was locked. I didn't have any possible explanation as to why this door was locked. It was opened about forty minutes ago. I had to look for someone to explain why the door was locked. So, I started looking around to see if I could find anyone who could give me the answers that I was looking for, then I saw a woman; she was seated at a spot on the church premises. So, I walked up to her. "Good afternoon... Do you know where Pastor Ruth and those people seated and waiting to be seen to by her had gone?" I demanded from the woman. She should be a woman in her late sixties. For a moment, she acted as if she didn't understand what I had said. I waited for her to talk, and at some point, started thinking that she probably wasn't hearing clearly. "Those people whom you saw here earlier had gone home." The woman responded. I was surprised. How could they all go home within forty minutes when they came to see pastor Ruth? I couldn't get my hands around it. "I thought the counseling was meant to end around 2:00 PM; I don't understand why they had to leave before time." I said. I needed more explanation, and I hoped the woman I was talking to wouldn't take as long as she took the first time to give me her response, and she didn't. "I heard that Pastor Ruth got an emergency call. She had to leave immediately. Honestly, she had done a lot more than she used to do today. She was here as early as 7:00 AM and started attending to those that came before the time. Some people come before the time to get a good spot in the queue, most likely a spot at the front. The counseling normally begins to be 9:00 AM, but she started by 7:00 AM, two hours earlier than she used to do in the past. That woman is a woman sent to us from heaven by God. I have never seen a woman devoting her time to God like Pastor Ruth does. How I wish my daughters were like her." The woman said. I was disappointed by what I had heard from the woman to whom I was speaking to. Again, I couldn't speak to Pastor Ruth about the apartment, even after coming for the third time to see her. But I had to be reasonable this time around; I didn't come earlier enough; there were people ahead of me, and she didn't know that I had come this time around. I had to be fair in my anger and frustration. This woman had a lot of good things to say about Pastor Ruth; I told myself that maybe I should sit with her and have a brief conversation with her before leaving. I then sat beside this woman. Silence prevailed for a moment as we stayed without speaking to each other for a while. I got some time on my hand; just staying for like thirty minutes to an hour wouldn't change much for me. "Are you waiting for anyone?" I asked the woman. Hearing my question, she smiled; it was as if she had just remembered something. "Yeah, I'm waiting for my boyfriend." She said. I had to look at her again closely to ensure I was sure about her age. She was happy, that's what I noticed, and I was happy for her. "You talked about your kids earlier, are you not married?" I asked her. "I used to be married, but we ended it sometime around six years ago. He was my first husband, it was a tough decision, but I had to let him go." She explained. It always interests me to hear stories like this, she was around her late sixties, divorced her husband six years ago, and said he was her first husband. It must have been a tough decision for her. "How long did you live with him before you divorced?" I asked. "Forty-one years." She responded. "Wow! That was almost a lifetime." I responded in astonishment. It surprised me that people could still have reasons to be apart even after being together for more than four decades. "I wasted a great part of my life waiting for him to change. There are some things about people that will never change. One common trait I see among young people makes me shake my head in disdain. Some of you go into marriage even after seeing a red flag; in your mind, you believe you can change this red flag after you've been married. I have learned that some women reasons for marriage is not about security or God ordained kingdom relationship, but the reason for marriage is about not feeling guilty about pre-marital sex. Fear of judgement or castigation. Really, they jump into situations unprepared and immature. Let me tell you when you're with a man, and he has some bad habits which he had always held on to since you met him, and during being in a relationship with him, he refuses to let them go, it would be the worst mistake of your life if you marry him. People like this will never change. If they didn't change before you married them, they will never change, even after you marry them." The woman explained. I've heard people say this severally before, and from what I've seen and from the ones I have experienced, I couldn't help but come to agree that this was true. When I started with Trent, it didn't take long before he showed his real self. I had stayed with him thinking that he would change since he was always remorseful whenever he did something wrong; he never changed. He just found ways to make me believe it was my fault or I provoked him. I tried my best to change who I was. I tried to be quiet, to be still, I tried not look at anyone, being with him I never knew what would trigger him. He continued getting worst. "I think I agree with what you've just said." I said to the woman. "They don't ever change. Mine cheated on me with my cousin a day before our wedding. I was so mad at him. He told me that they had been doing it since we met and had been struggling to stop, but it wasn't working. I didn't know how I forgave him. I had to put up with him lying and cheating all the time until she eventually got married and relocated with her husband. She would visit from time to time; I could see that how they looked at each other that never changed. I wasn't all that sure if they continued after she got married, but if the way they were looking at each other was something to pay attention to, they might have been still having relations even after she got married; she even had to joke during one of her visits that her first child looked like my husband. But my husband didn't stop there. He was seeing other women, and he was the most abusive man I had ever seen. There were even times he hit me. The only good thing I could pick out about him was that he was so good to his kids. He did all he could to make sure they were comfortable and weren't lacking anything, but that didn't stop him from doing the crazy stuff he was doing. One time, a lady sent me a text message, telling me she was pregnant for him. It was the most devastating violation he could do to me, the abuse was one thing I found ways to blame myself. The cheating was something I could pretend wasn't happening, but a baby! For all to see and know. That was a pill I could not swallow. I thought that as he got older, he would at least start changing and start becoming a better man, but I was so wrong. He never changed. He was a man that stood 6'3 with a well-build, broad shoulders long legs. He put me in the mind of the young man that played in the movie "Creed". To top it off he was a dynamic preacher. He knew the word of God, he could preach, play the organ and sing. Women were always finding ways to get his attention; I didn't know how I was able to put up with that. So, one day after feeling sick for a few days I decided I needed to go to the hospital. I had severe pains in my lower abdomen and could hardly walk. As I finished in the triage, the nurse asked me for a sample of my urine. She handed me a small cup and a wipe. Gave me instructions and escorted me down the hall to a nearby restroom. Once I was done, I handed the cup back to the nurse. As I waited in the emergency room that night, I begin to think about all that I had been through. While deep in my thoughts the doctor returned to the room to tell me my urine tested positive for chlamydia. Oh God! I had never been that mad before in my life. The day I found out; he had been away for two days after he said he was traveling for a work trip. I had to catch my breath. I was infected with a disease that my husband passed to me. I called up my best friend, I needed someone to talk to. She listened for a while been then interrupted to tell me she had been seeing him at this restaurant during lunch time with this popular woman pastor around my age. I had been putting up with him, but this time, I told myself I'd had enough. I called my kids together and spoke to them. They already knew their dad's lifestyle, and they didn't say anything to stop me from what I had decided to do. My eldest son told me to my face that I've endured a lot. He honestly didn't think any woman out there could put up for that long with their dad. His words made me emotional; even my son and his siblings were okay with me divorcing their dad. Throughout my entire marriage, I was always in and out of depression.

There were moments I thought about committing suicide because of how depressed I was. At first, I was staying with him because I loved him and was waiting for him to change, I could not believe that a man that preached the word of God and was so gifted in the church could be this horrible. I believed that I must have done something in my past life to deserve this. but with time, my reasons shifted. I was now there because of my kids, but if I had known that they would all support my divorce the way they did, maybe I would have just made that decision sooner than I did. I've thought deeply about why I couldn't leave him even when I knew it wasn't working; I realized that I resolved to love him more than he loved me. I did not want to ruin his life by exposing the real him to the church, they would never believe me. I've seen churches turn completely on the wife after she made accusations about what the husband was doing. I've seen the congregation embrace the husband, continue to listen to him preach with no anointing and never hold him accountable. I didn't have a job; I didn't have anything to my name, and I was living my life for him. I had a college degree, but I had to quit my job around when I was six months pregnant with my first child. I made a lot of sacrifices for this man whom I loved and got married to, I believed in him and was ready to continue being with him, but he ruined my life. When I eventually left him, I realized what a mess my life had been turned into. I lost my self-esteem and my identity. I lost faith in God. I never saw me surviving apart from him. After a while you can find normalcy in abnormal situations if you are not careful. I'm grateful for my kids, they helped me a lot because it was somewhat strange to adapt to the life of being alone after being married for forty-one years, but with time, I found out that it was possible. I learned how to love myself. I didn't need to get validation from anyone. Also, I now had a lot of time for myself. Life became more meaningful than it used to be; I kept regretting why I didn't make this decision earlier.' The woman explained.

"Wow! You really did endure a lot with him." I spoke. "Yeah, women do endure a lot. The truth is that if it is not working, it isn't working, and the more you continue to stay there, the more you get damaged in ways you would never expect. You might not even know that you're getting damaged. When you find yourself in a bad situation, when you've lived with this bad situation for a long time, you start feeling that there is no other way of living other than the bad way you've come to get used to. Being in a bad and abusive relationship strips you down to nothing. You feel there is no way out. You live in fear. You become their words. You believe it's your fault and deserve it. You coach yourself into just doing things right the next time. It has a way of messing with people's way of reasoning. For years, I continued going up and down, I couldn't make any decision, but I'm glad now. I've seen a better part of life which I've not thought I would ever see, and I would always say that if I had known, I would have made my move earlier." The woman explained. Her story was just another version of what I went through with Trent, but I think I was somewhat lucky because I didn't spend forty-one years with Trent just as this woman did with her husband. This woman's story affirmed that I made the right decision by leaving Trent and fighting for a way to get my life back. This woman stayed for forty-one years with her abusive and cheating husband, she must have been very badly damaged, but she was sitting next to me despite what she had gone through. God used her in that moment to give me a glimpse of myself and what my life could end up like if I didn't stand firm on my decision. If she could become happy after all the years that she spent in such a bad marriage, there was no way I wouldn't find happiness. Her story made me very resolute and firm in my decision. I looked at her for a moment; she was looking very beautiful and very happy. I smiled while I was looking at her, she then looked at me, she noticed that I was smiling. "What?" She asked me. I must have been lost briefly while smiling that I didn't know I was being too open with how I was feeling. "It's nothing." I responded. She then gave me a look that showed that she didn't believe in the response which I had just given to her. "Do you have someone in your life?" She asked me. "Yeah...." I responded but just realized that I was done with Trent. I've been so used to telling people that I was in a relationship that I had to really work on my response to make it reflect to my current state. "I mean no. I don't have any man now." I responded. She chuckled at the two responses that I had given. "You don't look sure of either of the answers that you gave." She said to me while she chuckled. "I'm sure. I don't have anyone. I used to have one that was like your ex husband. Hearing all that you've said about your ex husband in many ways. I could only be grateful that I made the right decision by leaving him. I wavered a lot before I was able to make up my mind." I explained. The woman nodded, she seemed to understand my situation. "Your ex, is he older than you?'' I asked her. I had asked this question because of the conversation I had with my sister and her roommate during the evening of Monday. They were talking about getting married to older men, and I realized that I haven't really thought about if I could date men way older than me. I've only been with Trent, and he was younger than me by about two years.

The woman I was speaking with started laughing after she heard my question. I stared at her as I wondered why she was laughing. After she was done laughing, she then looked at me. ''My man is twenty-eight.'' She said to me. I was surprised by what she had just said. I had to look at her again; she chuckled. ''Yeah, it is what you heard. He's twenty-eight, and he's the best thing ever in my life. Love sometimes comes from where we least expect. After my experience with my ex-husband, I never expected that I was going to fall in love anytime soon. I just wanted to stay healthy and live the best of my life, but love found me along the way.'' She explained while smiling. ''How long have you known each other?'' I asked her. ''Three years, but we've been together for two years. He's the nicest person in the world.'' She remarked. ''People who knew me were surprised how I found a younger man and all that. The truth was that I wasn't looking for love; it just happened. After I left my husband, I had a lot of time on my hand, I needed to get busy, and I needed to get fit. Being married to him made me lose my real self. I had to get myself back. So, I went to the gym. That was where I met my current man. It started like a mere acquaintance, gradually growing into a fire that started burning us up.'' She said and started laughing. While we were still talking, a car drove into the church premises and pulled up before us. The woman with me then got up from where she was seated. A guy quickly emerged from the car and walked up to her. He hugged her and kissed her cheek. ''I'm sorry it took long before I showed up." He said to her. "That's all alright." She said to him. "Meet my friend." She said while she tried to introduce me to him. I then stood up while looking at him. "Hello beautiful," he said to me with a warm smile. Before I could respond, he already took his attention back to her. He was so into her. I could see how much they loved each other. "I got to go now." She said to me. I nodded while smiling at her. They started walking to the car. She then stopped and looked at me. "My name is Roseline. I just remembered I didn't tell you my name." She said, and then they walked to the car. He opened the door for her, she went in, and he shut the door. He then drove the car, and they left. I watched them as they drove off the premises. Love has no bounds; these people still connected and were so much in love, despite their age differences. Roseline left her abusive marriage; she must have felt like she would have a chance at love for the first time. It was then that I realized God wants to heal us and take our brokenness and make us whole. He wants to heal us so that we can love again, trust again and feel beautiful again. I realized that while Rosaline had a right to be bitter, she made a choice to be better.

After Roseline had left, my reality dawned on me. I still had not met with Pastor Ruth, it's been weeks now. I was in the church, she was nowhere to be seen or found. I was losing hope. I honestly felt like I was never going to get the apartment.

chapter four

A COMBAT WITH THE PAST

t was Thursday evening. After I was done with work for the day, it was a long day because I was asked on short notice to stay back for an emergency meeting. By the time I got home, it was already 6:00 PM, so I had to move as fast as I could because I wanted to go to the prayer meeting that would be held that night, I planned to meet pastor Ruth after the prayer meeting to discuss the apartment once and for all. I told myself that it had to be tonight, no matter what. So, I quickly got into the shower. After I was done with my bath, I went to find something appropriate to wear. As I begin to apply my make-up the doorbell started ringing. My sister was not home; her roommate was not home either. So, I had thought that one or both might be at the door. I quickly finished my makeup, grab my purse, put my shoe on, and then started heading to the door. I planned to unlock the door and allow them in, and then start leaving the house.

I quickly got into the living room, I would normally turn off the light before leaving if I was leaving the house when nobody was in the house, but I wasn't going to turn out the light this time because I believed that people were coming into the house. I then got to the door and unlocked the door. I saw someone I was never expecting to see. I was so scared at first, but my fear gradually defused into surprise. Trent was standing right in front of me. How did he know where I was staying? Who told him? What was he going to do? I was dumbfounded as I stared at him standing before me. He then smiled at me; I could read the reason why he was smiling from his facial expression; from his smile, I could figure out he was saying, "you can't get away from me." At some point, I told myself I had to get it together and focus on my plan if he tried to grab me or hit me. I was going to fight like hell, he was about to see a new me. If there was anyone that should feel awkward, it should be him.I could be carrying anything on me. He should not believe that I would allow him to just abduct me in the open without putting up a fight. "It wasn't even difficult to find you," Trent said to me. It was his way of mocking me that I was trying to hide from him, but it wasn't difficult for him to find me. So, where are you going now? Do you already have boyfriend and we are still together?" Trent asked. The last question he asked sounded so disgusting to me. He was trying to make it sound like I was cheating on him. Throughout all the years that we were together, I never cheated on him. While I was with him, he was like the only one that existed to me. He made sure I cut off any dealings with any male friends. He hated all of them. He questioned my relationship with all of them consistently. "Did you ever kiss them? Did you ever give them some? Did you ever see their joint? Who's was bigger?" He would ask. This was practically every day of the relationship. I remember listening to Tank an R&B artist at the time one day in the car. While I was admiring the CD cover Trent became enraged, violently snatched the CD from my hand and threw it out the window. "I guess you want him too?" Trent asked. I never felt tempted to cheat but I always felt like I was treated as though I had. I would say I might as well do it he treats me like I'm doing it anyway, but I never had the guts. 'I got somewhere I'm going to; I don't have any time for this, with you tonight" I said to Trent. He didn't argue; he just remained quiet as I walked out of the door and locked the door. I started heading out; he had his eyes closed while taking a strong breath as I walked past him. "Oh goodness, I've missed your scent. You smell so damn good." He said to me; I just ignored him and continued where I was going. He followed me until he got a call from someone. I didn't know whom he was talking to on the phone, but I didn't care to know. I did hear him tell the person that he was coming as soon as possible. So, I felt relieved. I had been worried that he would follow me to the church. "I'll be back again," Trent said. I ignored him and started heading to where I would get a bus that would take me to where I was going. Trent quickly walked away. I didn't know where he parked his car, and I didn't care to know. I've heard people say that a when a black woman is fed up there aint nothing you can do about it. Nothing you can say to make her change her mind. When her cup if full she doesn't have the capacity to withhold anymore of anything. I believe this was the state I was in around that time.

I got onto the B35 bus headed to the church. The people were there walking the floor and praying. I hurried in and got on my knees. I went into prayer. The more I prayed the higher I went spiritually. Pastor Ruth prayed and cried out to the lord. She prayed as if it were her last time praying. "God help your people!" She cried out. I lifted my hands because I wanted to be one of the people God would help.

While the prayer was going on, Pastor Ruth called me to the altar. I was surprised. It was so out of the ordinary. I was never expecting her to call me to the altar. So, I couldn't just hide my surprise. I then walked up to the altar, not knowing what she would tell me. She then walked up to me and told me something that I had never thought about while I was in NEW YORK CITY. ''God is going to send you a husband who will love you. He'll give you peace and joy when you meet him; he'll love and cherish you more than any man had ever. Wait for him; he's coming.'' Pastor Ruth said to me. It was a prophecy. Honestly, I didn't know what I was going to say. It wasn't what I was thinking about around that time. I wouldn't say that love wasn't important, but I had a lot of stuff going on in my life; what mattered to me around that time was the apartment I was looking for. I just stood there, looking at her "Tell the Lord thank you!" She shouted. "Thank you, Lord!" I shouted. The people rejoiced in the church. I was ushered back to my seat. I was still in a state of shock, trying to figure out what was just said to me. The prayer service continued.

After the prayer meeting was finished, people waited for her to change. She was taken into the small office just like the last time. She changed what she was putting on and then returned to meet so many people that wanted to talk to her. The only problem with speaking to her now was that most of those coming to speak to her around that time wouldn't be able to get the privacy they wanted. I needed privacy; there was no way I would go there and try to start speaking about the apartment with her when there were many people around her. I had to allow her to attend to others. I had sat at a place where she wouldn't easily find me when the prayer meeting was going on, but she was able to locate me. Now that the prayer meeting was over, I was now waiting for others to be done with speaking to her before I would approach her so that we would talk about the apartment. She stayed there and talked to most of them. There were some she asked to come to see her in her office because of the nature of their problems; it wasn't something she could handle right there that she was standing with them. It was understandable because some counseling sessions normally take a very lengthy time before they conclude.

Once again, they swept her out and put her in her car. I watched as she was driven off the premises. I did not get to say hello. But I know she saw me, and I know she knew why I was there. It was so difficult to see this woman. After she left, I started heading out. For some reason, I was grateful that I had to come to the church that night it was inspiring. It made me feel that God had not forgotten about me and still found me worthy enough to be loved by someone. It was also the first time I did not let Trent change my mind; I don't know what would've happen to me if I didn't stick to my decision to go to prayer service that night.

It was over three weeks already, and I've been going to the church to see Pastor Ruth to discuss with her the apartment, but I was yet to have any conversation about it. Sometimes, when I sit and imagine it, it makes me feel frustrated in some ways. I didn't know I would still be staying with my sister and her roommate that long. While my sister might not be much of an issue, her roommate would need her own space back eventually; My sister had only moved in with her to work on getting herself established in New York. Now I was there with the same story. I was grateful that her roommate was sort of used to people coming to stay with her and working on establishing themselves. But I did not want to stay there for long. I was changing, I wanted to pray more and listen to gospel music. I wanted to be by myself. They had no idea of the internal war I was fighting daily. I seemed weird to them so I always felt like they would be happy when I got my own apartment.

On that Sunday, I was preparing to go to church. Pastor Ruth's church had gradually become a place I was now frequenting. I was enjoying the sermon there, I loved what was going on there and how the name of the lord has been exalted there, but most of the times that I was in there seated, my mind was always divided because I was yet to have any reasonable conversation with pastor Ruth about the apartment. We were yet to even talk about the apartment. "Are you sure this woman wants you in her apartment?" Nancy, my sister's roommate, asked me as I prepared for church. "I don't know, I must keep trying. I've put three weeks into it; I don't think it's okay to pull out now. We did not have a chance yet to say anything about it, so it makes no sense to walk away from everything when I have yet to get a straight rejection." I responded. "Some people might not reject you outrightly like they wouldn't tell you to your face that they don't like you. They'll continue playing around with you until you get tired of playing the game." Nancy explained. She was right in what she had said, some people are like that, but I didn't know why I couldn't stop trying to meet with pastor Ruth and then talk about the apartment. "You made a lot of sense, but I have no option now,"

I said to Nancy. "No, you do have a lot of options; you're just not looking at them," Nancy said to me. She had advised me about taking Trent back after I told them that Trent came around when I was about to go to church the other day. Nancy believed Trent must have regretted what he had done that led to me breaking up with him. I just smiled and didn't say anything to counter what she had said around that time. She was talking that way because she didn't know who Trent was. I believe that there are some people who will never change from the kind of people they are, I believe Trent was one of them. I will never forget the story Roseline told me about her husband. Her story proved that some people could never change. One will just be wasting precious time in their lives if they continued wasting their time waiting for someone that didn't want to change to change.

So, I was standing at the B35 bus stand, waiting for the bus to come. I was hoping that a bus would at least show up on time so that I would get to church early. I suddenly got a call from Trent. I wasn't going to pick up the call, but there was no need for me not to pick up the call. I had to come out clean with him. It was over between us; I had to make it clearer to him. It wasn't a case of just being mad at him; I wanted a new life away from being with him; I didn't want him anywhere around me again. I picked up the call and started talking with Trent. He then told me that he was downstairs waiting for me in front of the building where I was staying with my sister. I was surprised that he had driven from Tennessee early that morning for this, but I had to speak with him, and I didn't want him to know that I was about to get on the bus to go to church. So, I hung up immediately without saying anything to disclose my location. The bus had taken a bit longer to show up. While waiting at the bus stand, I felt someone standing beside me. I didn't look immediately since my eyes were fixed on the street that the bus traveled along. The person standing beside me didn't say anything to me. I knew he was a man, but I didn't look at him. But at some point, I noticed that he was looking at me or maybe looking at somewhere around me. I then took a brief look at the man beside me. I felt he was also waiting for a bus or so. I looked at his face with the intention of taking my eyes off him immediately, but I was surprised to see who it was. It was Trent. I was startled as I stared at him.

I didn't know how he found out that I was at the bus stop, but I later found out that Nancy had told him that I had left the house after he went to the door and demanded to see me. "What's up, babe?" He asked with a smile on his face; I wouldn't say I liked that smile too much. "Are you stalking me?" I asked Trent in anger. He laughed at me. I was so enraged by the way he was laughing at me. " I came here to get you. You are coming back to Tennessee with me." He said to me. "You mean you drove here from Tennessee this morning to come to ask me to come back with you?" I asked. "Yeah, that's how special you're to me. You know how I am. Whenever I want something, I will do whatever it takes to get it; it doesn't matter how far that very thing happens to be now when I'm longing for it." Trent explained he was so confident in himself. "Well, I won't be going back with you," I responded. "You know you can't stay away from me. You know you're not happy being away from me. There is no need to try to fight it this time. My car is over there; let's just go back to your sister house so you can pick up your things and we can leave." Trent said to me. He was feeling so entitled to me. He wasn't even seeing why I left him. I left him for a reason; he wasn't talking about correcting any of those reasons why I left him. Before now, I wasn't seeing this, but it was as if I'd become a different person with more sight than the person I used to be before. At that moment, I realized how much my mindset and my way of reasoning had changed. This was the man that would easily sway me with his words. Just a word from him made me change my mind about what I had planned on doing, but this time around, it was as if his words were annoying me. His words disturbed my spirit. He had been used to me coming back to him; he had been used to me feeling sorry for him and blaming myself. He was used to seeing me as belonging to him. Like as if I was his property that he could just lay claim on at will. I had never really said no to him whenever he was making demands from me, and even when he would be making demands, and I would be in the state of mind to allow him to have his way, he had always felt entitled and I just felt like I never had the energy or the will power to tell him no because I knew it would lead to hours of yelling and fighting. Sometimes being forced to lay pinned under him while he demanded answer to questions I knew nothing about. But that person whom he used to deal with back then was gone; She died. This person he was dealing with right now was new.

"I told you, Trent, it's over between us. I don't want to have anything to do with you. I had to move to New York City to get away from you. I thought that was clear." I explained to him. "If you have to move out from a place you love so much, where you had always planned to live your life, to another place just to stay away from me, what does it show to you?" Trent asked. I couldn't understand what he meant; he could see it from the looks on my face. You left Tennessee because of me. I know how much you love Tennessee; you have always wanted to live your life there and have your own family there. You told me several times about how much you love Tennessee and how you don't think there is any other place you can see yourself in other than Tennessee. Now, you had to leave this place which you cherish so much to come here just because of me; now tell me how that makes any sense." Trent demands.

"It shows how serious I am about not wanting to be with you ever again. It shows how much I would rather leave a place I love to go to a place where I have nothing just to have a chance to live my life free from all the hell you put me through." I responded in a firm tone while looking as serious as I could ever be. "No, I think you're seeing it from a negative angle. It shows how much you care for me. You abandoned what you love to escape from me; it means that it's so difficult to get me out of your mind. It shows that you always think of me, you always see me in your dreams and in your secret thoughts, long to be with me." Trent explained. I seriously felt like punching him in the face as I heard him talk. He sounded emotionally disturbed. "I think you're being delusional about yourself. Were we not in the same sick relationship? I could've lost my life dealing with you. That's it! I'm done with you and I'm done talking to you!", I regret all the years I spent waiting and thinking that you're going to become a better man. Still, even as we're talking right now, you just confirmed to me that I made the best decision of my life by deciding to walk away from this whole situation. I'll always see the time I wasted with you as the worst error of my life. I should have listened to my father. " I said to Trent. I could feel the impact of my words on him. He looked angry, but I knew he couldn't lay a finger on me there. We were in a public place; there were people everywhere around there. Trent remained quiet for a moment. He must have been thinking about all I had said, and it might be dawning on him that I was pretty much serious with everything I had said. He probably had not seen me this way before. I wasn't that girl that would start crying as soon as I started talking. There were times I would cry in front of him as a result of the things he was doing and saying, but I wasn't that person again. While we were still there, a bus showed up, and without saying anything to Trent, I got on the bus and was hoping I was done with him for good. I then walked to a seat at the back and sat there; then I saw someone walk in and sit beside me. Trent was going to follow me to church. I wasn't expecting him to get on the bus, I had expected him to walk back to his car and leave after I had made it clear to him that I didn't want to have anything to do with him, but he got on the bus with me and was now seated beside me. I didn't want anyone bothering me in the church. I didn't' want anyone to see me with him. I was going to church for something very important; I didn't want anyone in my business or Pastor Ruth thinking I was with him and change her mind about giving the apartment to me.

"I hope you're not coming to church with me?" I asked with an angry look on my face. "I asked you to come with me you said no, so I'm going with you!" Trent responded. I was so mad at him. This was becoming too much, and I was finding it difficult to tolerate him. I then tried to get up and go to another seat, but he held me back and made sure I didn't leave the seat I was in. I struggled to feel myself, he held me down. This was who he was, he always loved to have his way at all costs, but I wouldn't let him to this time. We struggled, with me trying to get up and him trying to hold me down. For a moment, I didn't mind the people on the bus. The people around us were looking. We were soon becoming somewhat loud, so I had just to give in because I saw that he didn't care. I wished someone would at least intervene. No one did. Again, I was embarrassed, angry and feeling powerless.

"Why did you leave me?" Trent asked while the bus was moving. I gave him a staring look and then took my gaze away. He had just asked me one of the dumbest questions I heard that day. How could he ask me why I left him? He knew exactly why I left him, so it was a rhetorical question for him to ask. He was trying to use his masculine nature to suppress me and make me do his bidding. It was something I'd seen so many times before, so it wasn't new to me. I didn't say anything to respond to the question Trent had asked me. "You are coming back with me. You're up here sleeping in a back room on a kid size bed, with all those people in that house. Is that how you want to live?" Trent said. "I'll rather die than go back to you, Trent. It's still over. No matter what you say, no matter what you do, It's sill over between us." I fired at him. "I no longer love you! I spoke. "Oh, I get it, you left me to come up here to be with the nigga you cheating on me with, that's why you talking to me like that. But I will tell you this, if I can't have you nobody can! And I will die on that fact". Trent insisted. "When you called me this morning, I knew you'll be like the devil that would try to hinder me from going to church today," I said to Trent. "We both know you always wanted one of those goofy ass church niggas. That's why you so stressed to go to church all the time. He must be at that church, who is he? Is he the organist, preacher? Oh, maybe he's the pastor. But we gone find out today who he is, I'm breaking his face and you still going back with me" Trent insisted. "I think it is time to call the cops on you; this is getting past ridiculous. I want my freedom!" I said, almost yelling on the bus. "You can take my phone and give those cops the call. I don't care. If you decide to go to church, I'll follow you there, and make sure I embarrass you there. You know me; you know how petty I could be if I want to become petty." Trent said proudly. Yeah, he was a very petty person. I don't think I've seen someone as petty as Trent, but I wouldn't allow his pettiness to deter me. "We've been through a lot, and you just want to throw all that into the wind; no, I'm not going to allow that to happen; you are not going to have me out here looking like less than a man!" Trent said while giving me a fierce look. I avoided his gaze because I didn't want anything to do with him. Having him around me was beginning to become repulsive. Since I got to NEW YORK CITY, bus rides used to be one of the best moments of my days. They always allowed me to clear my mind and process my life as I traveled from one location to the next. But having Trent around me ruined what should have been one of my beautiful moments of the day.

I argued a lot with Trent on the bus; I couldn't help it. He made me look like I was out of control, but I was in full control, I was taking a stand, this was new for me. The bus finally got to where I would be getting off at. It was relieving that I was going to be free from being confined around him. Immediately I got up to leave the bus, he got up too and left the bus. He intended to force his decision to make me not go to church on me; he wasn't getting off the bus because he had the intention to follow me to the church. Immediately we got off the bus; I started walking as fast as I could, then he followed immediately, trying to hold and stop me, then I noticed a lady walking ahead of me; eating some peanuts. I'd never met her before this day, but she suddenly turned and looked at me. "Good morning." She said to me. She looked very inviting. I tried to engage her in a brief conversation even though I was in haste, and our conversation turned out to be kind of beneficial to me. "Where are you going to?" The lady asked me. She looked stronger and older, and she looked like a no-nonsense kind of person; Trent became subdued for a moment as he saw me talking with her. "I'm going to the church." I said to her. She smiled at me. Oh that's so nice, you don't see too many young folks going to church, I'm going to church too, how about we walk together?; This lady asked me. I never told her that I was in the middle of a struggle with Trent or that Trent was trying to force me into what he wanted me to do, and she wasn't on the bus to have seen what happened between me and Trent on the bus, whoever told her that I needed help around that time, I will never know. I accepted the offer immediately. She looked very happy as she tried engaging me in a conversation while we walked to the church. Trent followed quietly from behind without saying anything, as he couldn't say anything about her being with me. We had walked for about a minute when this lady suddenly stopped and turned to look at Trent. Trent wasn't expecting the looks he was getting from her; it was sudden, so he just stopped, looked at her briefly, and took away his gaze. The looks on her face were intimidating; he was intimidated by how she was looking at him as he didn't know what she was going to say to him. He had heard our conversation as he followed behind us. I knew he would be eavesdropping to see if I was going to tell her anything about him, but I didn't, she didn't even ask me anything about him, this must have also been why Trent didn't expect the way she suddenly turned around and was looking at him. "Don't ever try to stand in the way of someone going to church. God does not like that." The lady said to Trent. Trent remained quiet; he didn't know what to tell her; I could bet that he didn't know that, that was what she was going to be telling him. She didn't see him try to stop me; maybe she saw a vision about it, but I could see how subdued Trent was." Stop a person from going to a night club or doing drugs. But don't you ever stop them from going to church." The lady said. The lady had waited for a moment to see if Trent could say anything, but he didn't; he couldn't even look at her face. So, we continued walking to the church while continuing our conversation. Talking to her was very inspiring. She was talking from an angle that I had never thought of. She told me many things that made me believe and that I was doing the right thing at that time. Doing the right thing will not always be easy. Once one wants to do the right thing, there are always chances that many things will try to come up and get in their way. Good things never come easily. For one to achieve something good, one might need to struggle for it; one might need to work very hard for it. Quitting will always seem easier than sticking to the task at hand. During that very time that one is working hard for it, a lot of things might come up and try to militate against all the work that this person working hard for it is putting up to be able to make things move. Most of the things this lady spoke to me about were happening in my life. I told myself this was the kind of person I would like to have around me. When you're someone with a target in life, like eagles. Eagles have vision. Eagles fly alone at high altitudes. Eagles ae fearless and never surrender to the size or strength or its prey. Eagles are tenacious. Eagles possess vitality. You have to be an eagle to find an eagle." She spoke. This is just what I needed. I planned to sit with her when we got to the church and hopefully we could exchange numbers. I always enjoyed having conversations with people that were much older than I. I always felt like it was an opportunity for me to gain wisdom and deeper insight.

Then we got to the church building. I went ahead of her as I begin to go into the church, and she followed behind me. Trent was behind us, but he looked distracted. After she talked to him about him trying to stop me from going to church, he seemed off; he wasn't listening to our conversations anymore as he was following behind us and wallowing in whatever thought was in his mind. I didn't even understand why he was still following us, he should have just turned and stopped following us, but he just continued following.

When we got to the church, Iwas just about to step into the church. I decided to look at the lady following behind me because it seemed she had reduced the pace at which she was walking with me immediately we got closer to the church building. I was waiting for her so we could walk in together, but as I turned around, I couldn't find her. I was lost for a moment as I couldn't make sense of what was happening. After a moment of being lost and then collecting myself, I went back a bit to where we had walked past to see if she had turned or maybe she had followed another route, but she was not there. Just as she emerged from out of nowhere she vanished into nowhere. Trent was also confused because he had thought saw that I was speaking and walking with her, he wasn't paying attention to her, but he knew that she had been ahead of him with me. I looked around to see if there was anyone I could at least ask if they saw her, but there was no one I could say anything to. This lady practically vanished into the air without any single trace of her. I had to ask myself whom I had been talking to all this while. While I stood there thinking about what had just happened, I tried to replay each step in my mind. I wasn't going to talk to her. I had planned just to walk past her without saying anything to her. In NEW YORK CITY, people mind their business, and I gradually started getting used to it. But she was the one that drew my attention to her; she greeted me and then engaged me in a conversation, and then she had to talk to Trent about him trying to get in my way from going to church. She talked to me as though she knew I needed help in that moment. It was as if God sent an angel to my rescue. "Did you know where that lady went to?" Trent asked me. He just pulled me out of my thought. He knew that I was searching for her; I didn't know what he wanted to hear from me when he knew that she had vanished from us. Maybe he was frightened. I didn't give him any response. "I knew something wasn't right the moment she walked up to me and said that stuff said. She must have been a ghost or something close to that. You haven't been here long, and you're already making friends with these crazy people in New York." Trent said. He was trying to get me to say something, but I didn't have any time for him right now. I just turned around and then started walking to the church building. I walked into the church. Trent quickly followed behind me. He ensured he followed me to the place where I wanted to sit. He sat beside me. The service was already on by the time we came. So, I had to sit where it was comfortable for me and not too far from the pulpit. The place I would have preferred to sit had been occupied by people who had come earlier before Trent, and I showed up in the church. I noticed Pastor Ruth looking at me as I went to sit with Trent sitting beside me. "You decided to come to church, and you came late. Even God would be mad at you." Trent said while he tried to aggravate me. I didn't respond to what he said. There was no need to argue with him while in the church. The sermon was going on; I had my attention so fixed on the sermon. At this point, it would be safe to say that I wasn't just going to the church because I wanted to talk with Pastor Ruth. Yes, I wanted to talk her about the apartment, but I was also there because I wanted to experience God. I didn't know if God was drawing me closer to himself using the apartment. My spiritual life was getting better than it was before I had been praying more than I did before . I had less distractions. Praying was always a burden; Trent didn't want me praying too long he felt like I was ignoring him. Even when we went to church down south. He never enjoyed the service, he would just complain about who I was looking at or talking too. He especially didn't want me to engage in any conversation with a man. So, I always struggled to connect spiritually because I was always at war with Trent even in church. The sermon must have been in session for up to twenty minutes before I came in. I've been in this church for a while now, I've listened to several sermons, and I've known the duration most of the sermons said in the church last. So, it didn't take as long as it used to take in the past before the sermon ended. Then it was now time for an alter call. The alter call was a time when the pastor would make an appeal for those wanting to commit their lives to God or those wanted to pray before god, I made my way down to the alter. I poured out my heart to God. I cried out to God to deliver me from guilt and shame. Guilty for not following his voice and the shame of what I thought people were thinking of me. I prayed for a release in my spirit. I was feeling so oppressed. I was feeling overwhelmed I asked God to even deliver Trent from that spirit that was driving him. He stood by me as I prayed, he wasn't praying he was looking at me as if he was witnessing a new person emerge. He had never seen me crying and praying with such power and passion. But this was growth. I had found my weapon and my strength in prayer.

Apart from talking to me around when we walked into the church, Trent surprisingly remained quiet throughout the service. At some point, I had thought he had dozed off, but I always found him awake. Looking around the church trying to see if someone was looking at me. He was quiet and calm. Sitting up mostly looking but not saying a word.

The service soon ended, and Ruth was taken to the small office where she would have to change into something else. People waited for her as always. I also waited. So, after she came out, she took time to greet and talk to those waiting for her. She then started looking around; it was as if she was searching for someone; she then sighted me. She then looked at Trent, and she smiled. I had seen her few times to know how she normally smiles, but this particular smile was overly extended. She then walked to where we were standing. I greeted her to cut off the attention she had channeled on Trent, who seemed to find the looks she gave him somewhat interesting. He believed that Ruth had endured the union between me and Trent. "Apostle, this is Trent, my sister's husband." I heard a very familiar voice say from behind me. It was the voice of my sister. I looked at her immediately and then at Ruth; it was as if something was going on that I didn't know. I was surprised to see my sister because I never thought she would show up at the church. After listening to what my sister had said, Ruth seemed to take a closer look at Trent. "Oh, hello." She said to him while she pulled down her glass to get a better view of him.

Going home that day, I sat on the same bus with Trent. He was calm when he tried to engage me in some conversations, but I didn't want to have a conversation with him. I ensured I killed every conversation he was trying to put through right before it went through. By the time the bus dropped us off. Trent announced that he would be leaving to go Tennessee. He then asked if I wanted to come with him, and I told him that I didn't want to go with him. He didn't ask me again. He just got into the car and drove off.

I was going to go home, but I just couldn't. I had to take a walk. I knew that my sister and her roommate would be at home, so I didn't want to get involved in a conversation with them just yet. My sister introduced Trent as my husband to Ruth even after she knew the situation of things between me and Trent. My sister's roommate had always told me that I had a lot of alternatives and that I wasn't making good use of them. She wanted me to go back to Trent; I was now understanding where my sister's roommate got the idea of me going back to Trent from, my sister had to have discussed my situation with her. I then thought about what Ruth had said to me about getting a good husband that would love me. After she had called me to the pulpit to tell me that she saw a good man coming to be my husband, I never really thought about it. After I left the church during the day, I had a lot of things going on in my mind. Marriage, at that point, was never something that I was thinking about. How could I think about marriage when I was already married? Then, Ruth smiling at Trent. Did she smile at him because she had thought that he was the husband that she was talking about? I thought she was a prophet of God. Why didn't she see him for who he really was? Was he going to fool her too? I thought to myself. He had a way about him, he was always so nice to everyone on the outside but behind closed doors he was completely unhinged. After I'd walked around for like fifty minutes, I decided to return home because I knew that my sister and her roommate would be waiting to hear about how things went between me and Trent.

It was night already. Sunday had been a quiet day for me. Since I showed up in NEW YORK CITY, Sunday had always been a day I had always had for myself. It was time for me to go to bed. I was already lying down, and while waiting for sleep to take me off, my mind went through some of the things that had happened earlier that day. My mind was focused for a moment on the lady that was eating peanuts whom I had spoken to until I got to the church.

My mind also went to Ruth smiling at Trent. I tried to imagine what she was thinking when she was smiling at Trent; maybe she thought that he was the man she had told me about would be my husband. I shook my head in negation because I knew that Trent was never someone I was going to accept back into my life. I was yet to see anything about him that would have been reason enough for me to change my mind about him. I was already feeling sleepy; I must have even slept for a moment, then my phone started ringing. This woke me from the short-lived sleep I had drifted into. "Hello," I said as I positioned the phone to my ear, I didn't even look at the screen before answering the call to know who was talking to me on the phone. "Are you sleeping?" The voice from the other end said. Hearing her voice, the sleep in my eyes suddenly disappeared. It was the voice of someone I had never expected to call me. Ruth. I quickly sat up because I knew there was no way she was going to call me if she didn't have something important that she was going to speak to me about. Of course, we met each other at the church earlier that day. Although I couldn't get to meet her to have a one-on-one discussion with her, we at least stood close to each other for nothing less than a minute. "Good evening, Apostle." I greeted. "Good evening, daughter." She said to me.

"I'm sorry that I had to call you at this hour, but when God says something, as an instrument, we do exactly what God says we should do without trying to bring our flesh into it. One thing I know, if I don't know anything else is God does not lie. He is faithful to his word. The enemy wants to make us think that God will not do what he says because our circumstances don't match us being blessed or God even thinking about us. But I want you to know God does not lie". Ruth explained over the phone. It was as if she was preaching a sermon to me, but I had this feeling that there was something she wanted to say to me; there was no way she was going to call me and say some random stuff while I waited to hear the main reason why she had called me, she later said, "the prophecy still stands, God is going to send you a husband." She said to me. I believed this was the main reason why she was calling me. To remind me about the prophecy, she had called to remind me about the prophecy she had given me before. Looking back, I believe she called me to see where my mindset was really at. Did I still believe her, did I trust her. Would I look at her as a false, inaccurate prophet. "How will God send me a husband when I already have one, Apostle? I asked. She was quiet for a moment; she must have remembered my sister introducing Trent as my husband. "The prophecy still stands" she said. "Can you come to my house, maybe at 7:00 PM tomorrow?" She asked me. I was surprised. This was the first time she wanted to see me personally, and it wasn't at the church. I didn't know the address; I wasn't going to ask. I was going to wait for her to give it to me if she was serious about me meeting her. Ruth gave me the address. So, it was a deal; I would be going to see Ruth in her house by the evening of the next day. Finally, things were about to change.

chapter five

DEAL OR NO DEAL

t was about 6:55 PM when I showed up at Ruth's place. I would have shown up at her place about thirty minutes earlier, but I decided to stroll around her neighborhood to kill time even though I showed up earlier; this was to make it look like I wasn't desperate. By the time I walked in, she was already waiting for me.

"I don't think you had an issue with getting here," Ruth said. "Not at all. The address wasn't complicated." I responded. "I'm just saying, because you haven't been in this city for too long." said Ruth. "I understand," I responded. "So, man you showed up with at the church the other day, he's your real husband?" Ruth asked me. "Yeah, something like that, it's a long story". I responded. My response looked funny to her, so she chuckled briefly. "How long have you been with him?" She asked me. "Too long, I met him my last year in college. It started off nice. He showed me a few signs that I ignored. I hoped that he would change. He went in the military, I thought it was a good idea. I figured the military would make a man out of him. I remember going to visit him on family and friends day, on my way to see him, he called and instructed me to say I was his wife when I came. I agreed and everything else happened quickly. Next thing I know we were getting married before he was headed to A.I.T advanced individual training. When that was completed, I was moving to Tennessee. While in Tennessee the arguing increased met with the fights. To be honest I didn't realize it was abusive. I just thought we were not getting along. Things between us became worse. It was not until one evening things got violent. The glass coffee table was broken in pieces, the television was shattered and I was held down in the kitchen on the floor for what felt like an eternity. I thought I was going to end up as a statistic. I made up my mind I was leaving. I called my parents while he was at work and told them if they wanted to see me alive, they needed to come get me. I left and a never looked back. I was young and in experienced. I believed I was doing the right thing at that time. You know being in church you want to do what is right. But the whole situation was wrong for me from the start. "I'll walk you through this situation," Ruth said. "If you let me, I will help you get through this. Ruth said.

"Honestly, I don't want to go back to him. I want to stay away from him. The only reason I haven't filed for a divorce is I can't afford it yet. But as soon as I'm situated that's what I will do". I spoke. "The lord will provide for you". Ruth stated. "I know one thing he better not try that mess anymore." "You've come to the right place to be delivered". Ruth said to me. Silence prevailed among us for a moment. I wasn't sure if it was okay to divulge all of what I just spoke. So, I stood quiet for a moment.

"What about the apartment?" I asked her. I had to ask her now that I had gotten the opportunity. For weeks, I've been making countless efforts, but none have been fruitful. She remained quiet for a moment and then said, " I'm not ready to sublet this apartment. I was going to buy house, but we need a new place to worship. I only pay $288.00 per month here. I'm not going to get any debt before I get a new place for the people to worship. "She explained. What was I just hearing? I thought. I was so devasted. This entire time I have been on a wild goose chase. "Maybe a year from now I will be ready, but sorry honey no time soon. When the lord say so, I will, until then I will be still. Ruth said. "Oh wow, my family friend led me to believe that you were ready now, that's what led me to the church, that's the reason I continued to come". I said fighting back the tears. "You don't understand I need to get out from where I'm staying, it's not a good place, I need to be able to pray and think, I been through a lot". I spoke. I was almost pleading with her. She remained calm. "The Lord will provide. Be ye anxious for nothing".

I left her home felling a sickening in my stomach. I returned to my sister's place. I told them about the latest development with Ruth. They were surprised that I had been on this wild goose chase only to be disappointed again. I then told them how Ruth tried to convince me that things would work out for me. Nothing she said made sense after that meeting. "She's a false prophet". My sister said. "How is she going to tell you God is going to send you a husband and you have one? Then why did she tell you to keep coming to her church and she knew all the while she had no intentions to give you her apartment. Something is not right with that lady. But do what you want. You know everything. She said sarcastically. "You might as well go back with Trent, try to work things out, it can't be that bad". She stated.

While we were still talking my phone started ringing. I took my phone out my purse and then looked at my screen; it was Trent. I wondered why he was calling.

''Where are you now?'' Trent asked me. ''At home. The time is almost 9:30 PM; where do you expect me to be right now?'' I asked. ''I'm downstairs with my friends; we're waiting for you so you can come back home with me.'' Trent said. ''I told you, Trent that I can't continue in whatever you want. I'm done, Trent. This is not what I signed up for, I got every right to pull out when things don't seem to be going the way we had both agreed it would be going.'' I explained. ''You seem always to forget that we're married. "I'm not your boyfriend, Toya. I'm your husband. You're my wife. We can't just breakup like that. You can't live up there like you a single woman. You trying to embarrass me and make me look crazy in front of my friends. Get your ass down these stairs now. '' Trent yelled. I don't care about your friends. Do they know all of what you did and all of what you put me through,'' I said to him. Trent tried all he could to persuade me to come with him, but I stood my ground; I made it clear to him that I was not going with him. My mental health had been so stable since I stayed away from him, and I was still working on fixing my life; I was not going to put myself back in the very thing I worked so hard to get out of.

Trent left and went back home without me. After the day he had followed me to church, I doubted that he had gone back home; he had friends in NEW YORK CITY, and he must have hung around with his friends. I never liked to get into an argument with him in front of his friends, but they were very much involved in our relationship in ways I was not comfortable with. I think a man mature for marriage should be able to set clear boundaries between his marriage and between the relationships he is having with friends or relatives. I'm not a fan of people leaving what they used to enjoy doing before they got married just because they got married. Marriage would be very boring if one has to leave what they saw as fun just because they got married. The only very important thing is to set boundaries. A married person should at least have boundaries; they should know the limits which they're not meant to cross. In the case of Trent, he rarely ever had limitations. Many things about him were off; I didn't know how I could endure the way I did, for the time I did.

The next day was Tuesday; I was at work when I got a call from a friend in Tennessee. She asked me how things were with Trent and me and I told her that I was sticking to my decision of not going back to him. She was surprised because I would always change my mind after I insisted that I wouldn't be with him again. This time, I was acting so differently from what she had known of me. I sounded surer and more convicted than I ever sounded before. I told her that all the previous times I returned to him was out of fear mainly of what he would do to himself. I told her that I didn't realize he was an abuser until I got away. The extreme jealousy, possessiveness, the unpredictability it was too much. His antiquated beliefs about the role of a wife was not equal to my beliefs. I could no longer bare this burden. I told her the old me died; she was talking to the new me.

chapter six

NOTHING IS FOR FREE

The day was finally here. I was moving. So many things changed between my sister and Nancy. My sister decided that it was best for her to leave from Nancy's place. We decided we should get an apartment together. We could go half on everything. I knew staying in Ruth's apartment would come with a cost; yeah, it would come with a cost, and it wasn't a cost that I was ready to pay. Besides what would that be like would that be like living in the Pastors apartment. We set our place up nice. I was working and beginning to put the pieces of my life together.

Trent didn't stop making efforts to get back with me. With time, he found out that I had moved. He had got deployed to Korea. I didn't have to worry about him showing up harassing me. He was doing all he could to make sure when he returned to the states, we would be together, it seemed the more I stayed away from him, the more I found more resolve to be away from him. I found another part of life that I had long for. I found peace with life. Instead of being in a relationship that would make you almost lose your sanity. It was better to be alone. Many women fears being alone, they say" the clock is ticking". Is it really?

Society creates unrealistic time frames of when things should happen in a woman's life. Women internalize these already created time frames. They begin to set their goals and aspirations around what already exist. It's okay to aspire to these pre-set goals. However, what happens when life is not in synced with what you have planned. These plans never seem to include pain, uncertainty or consistent hard work. When life alters the plans one can begin to lose hope. I had plans for myself. My life certainly did not align with my plans. I had to figure out how to adjust to unwanted pain, to the reality of uncertainty and develop a way to use all my realties as fuel for survival.

Apostle had made the connection for my sister and I to get the apartment. Not realizing early on that this connection would come with a price. She saw it as if she was doing me a huge favor, and there were things I would have to do for her, even when I didn't want to do these things or when I was not in the mood to do them. I just had to do them to make her happy or to be obedient to leadership.

This night, I was so exhausted I just needed a moment of sleep. I had done a lot that day, and I was exhausted. I had already assisted Ruth in doing a lot of stuff, throughout the week and it had exhausted me. I also had some work that I had brought home with me. It wasn't a habit I enjoyed doing, but I couldn't avoid this one. I know how bringing work home could rob people of the family moments that they should enjoy with their loved ones. "Too much of anything is not good". My grandmother would often say to me. "You must have a healthy balance. Take time to rest and reset. I never thought about this until I begin to feel completely overwhelmed. I didn't want to be a workaholic. I dedicated a lot of time to my work, but I made sure I had limits to the time I was dedicated to my work. I made sure I was at work at the normal hours, which I should be at work; I returned home at the normal hours, which I should return home, and never returned home to work unless when it was very necessary.

So, this particular night, I was so exhausted. I just needed to sleep. Then I got a call from Apostle. When I saw the phone ringing, I went for it; it was her. I just couldn't ignore her call; at this point in my life, she had become part of those whom I could never ignore calls. I used to think if God was himself calling. If I ignored her, it was like ignoring God. So, I spoke with Apostle on the phone, and she told me she needed my help in preparing her sermon, which she was going to be preaching the next evening. Honestly, I felt like crying at this point because my whole body was exhausted, my body was asking for rest, but she wanted it done that night. She always had a lot of preaching engagements, and it had gradually become my responsibility to be prepare those sermons for her, especially the introductory part of it." Write it good" she said. Just like you write yours. She spoke. "She had allowed me to speak a few times at the church and the members were really taking to the messages I would share. At first when she made this request

I was honored. Wow I thought, this is a powerful woman, and she wants me to write for her. Then it turned into if this woman is a powerful why does she want me to write for her. "I'll get you a laptop which will help you with your work," Ruth added. I think she must have perceived how disturbed I was that night; bringing up the laptop might have been a way to make me feel better.

A year had passed, Ruth was now enrolled in school. She was working on a degree in theology. I was hit with another request from Ruth to look at an assignment that was going to be due soon. Initially she would say to me that she didn't have time to work on it. "I can't think about this assignment and hear from the Lord." Ruth would say. "I need you to help me do this, God is going to bless you for helping me. " Ruth said.

This faithful evening, I had something I wanted to talk to Apostle Ruth about. There was no way she wouldn't end up finding out. I've been thinking about this for a while, and at this point in my life, I believed it was time for me to do something about it. I decided to give her a call. "Hi Apostle, how are you?" I asked. "Oh I'm blessed of the Lord." She responded. "How are you, normally you don't all me she said, too scared I'm going to ask you to do something. She casually said. "I wanted to talk to you about something" I said. "Oh really, I was in the middle of setting up my calendar. It's getting closer to the "prayer clinic" and I must put some things in order. The prayer clinic was a time when pastors would come and preach, teach and pray. There would be daytime sessions and nightly services for a week. Apostle would usually close out the service at the end of the week. I'm going to need you to help me with this conference. I need to hear from God. It's a lot that goes into these things. I need you to contact the Pastors, send emails and make some calls. I need you to go shopping for me because I need some new clothes for the conference. I need some new glasses as well. Will you be able to put a letter together from the desk of the Apostle. I want that to go into the program. Ruth said. I could feel the anxiety rising in my stomach. I felt to vomit. "So, you were going to tell me something. Ruth said. She said all she had to say about the forthcoming prayer clinic in which she would be hosting, but still had what I wanted to tell her in her mind; it must have dawned on her again that I had called her.

''I've been thinking about this for a while. At this point in my life, I think it's the right thing to do. When I came to NEW YORK CITY, my plan was to get myself together. I didn't have a very clear view of what I wanted to do. But now, I think I can see clearly what I want for myself." I said and then paused for a moment. "Okay, I'm waiting to hear what you want for yourself," Ruth demanded. "I want to go back to school. "As a matter of fact, I already applied to the graduate program. I know it will be different this time because my circumstances are different. I didn't know how I was able to graduate from college because of the too much emotional stress I had with Trent..." I was still talking when Ruth interrupted me. "Wait... I'm not trying to interrupt what you're saying, but the Lord is not releasing you to go back to school. It's not the season. You are already working, and you work for this ministry. The Lords work comes first". Ruth explained. "You must be careful putting what you want to do before God's work. He will fix it so that you will end up with nothing. Your greatest fear will come upon you if you are not careful". I hated what she had just said, how did any of what she had said make sense. Why does God not want me to go back to school. I thought. I was so confused. It was like everything I wanted for myself that did not involve her,

God was not in it. "You may not like what I'm saying but it's not me saying it, its God". Ruth said.

I kept silent on the phone. Another dream being shattered. I didn't honestly know which situation was worse being with Trent or being under this religious cult with Ruth. "Don't you realize its souls to be saved through the prayer clinic. Ruth said. "I told you that I was going to walk you through this journey, you were so used to making bad decisions, that's how you ended up with that man. Had you known me, that would have never happened to you, you must trust me". She spoke. "Do you trust me? She spoke. "Yes, I trust you, but my sister said you are a false prophet." I spoke. "Well, who do you say that I am?" Ruth said. Silence hit the line. "Who do you say that I am!" Ruth shouted. "I say you are an apostle. A woman of God" I said. I never wanted her to think I didn't believe in her or that she was not in my corner. She always had the upper hand on me because she was the leader. She had always been the one that ended up influencing whatever decision I was making. Everything was good between us if it wasn't something that made me happy.

"As I was saying, I already registered for school. I submitted all of my documents; I'm already accepted. I got my acceptance letter today. That was what I wanted to tell you." I announced. I just had to go straight to the point despite what she just said because then I would be rebuked for not telling her or "operating in secret" like she would like to say. Ruth remained quiet for a moment. She didn't reply to what I had said immediately; I just wondered why she was quiet. "You've been helping me with my sermons, my schoolwork, and I told you I need your help with the prayer clinic plus you go to work. How will you be able to mix all that with going for your Masters' degree?" Ruth asked. Honestly,

I felt so disappointed by the question which she had just asked. I was already seeing a side of her that I had never noticed initially. I wouldn't be wrong if I concluded that she was being selfish. She was always putting herself and her interest first before anything that had to do with me. Whenever it was something that had to do with me, she would always look for how to downplay it and then prioritize hers over mine. I was talking about me going back to school and obtaining my Masters' Degree; I had expected her to be happy for me that I would finally be going back to school. It wasn't an easy decision for me to make. It took time before I was able to build up myself mentally for this, but she had to put her church work and her studies first before mine. I remained quiet; I didn't want to say something that would end up becoming wrong to her ears. "I almost forgot. You know that I'm gradually putting things together to establish my school. You said that you're going to help me get that done. You know how busy my schedules are sometimes; there is no way this is going to work without your full input." Ruth said. "you said you're planning to establish a school two to three years in the future. We still got time. My master's degree program wouldn't last up to two years. "I never said three years, maybe two to two and half years," Ruth said. "It's still the same. As far as your sermon and schoolwork, I never said I would stop assisting you with them. I'll look for how to manage my time and do all of them." I explained. "I'm just worried that you'll be stressing yourself out doing too many things at a time," Ruth said. This sounded like a damage control because as she said this, I felt something come over me. I honestly didn't find any sincerity in what she had said, It was mixed with all of what she wanted and none of what I wanted. It was filled with what God doesn't want for me because I must do all of what she wants me to do. These conversations were starting to feel typical. It felt like I was dealing with Trent just in the form of a woman as a Pastor this time.

Ruth and I had a lengthy conversation about my plans to start attending school; we talked about the college and which programs I would be enrolling in. She felt like the class hours was a bit late and too demanding; I told her that I wanted it in the evening time so I can still work and pay my bills. I told her it would be convenient for me because I could leave from work catch a train straight to the school. I told her that my classes were during the week and on Saturdays. I had to miss mid-week prayer and Saturday 5 am prayer. She was not in agreement with any of what I had stated. She saw a lot of reasons in my decision to disagree with. I listened to her talk for about an hour. I felt it was time for me to retire. I had to get up early the next day. I said goodnight and ended the conversation.

chapter seven

THE DISTANT ADMIRER

Class was in session. I was in my third year of teaching. I had completed two graduate degrees for myself and two degrees despite Ruth's constant demands on my time. School had always been a haven for me. I loved to learn and be a part of meaningful discussions. School was like another world. A place where objectives were clear and obtainable. A place where I felt like I belonged. I don't know how I was able to complete two graduate programs, while doing all of Ruth coursework for her degrees in theology, honestly giving up was easier. Whenever I enrolled in school, she decided she needed to pursue a graduate degree as well. It led me to typing papers, sermons and driving her to her school for her evening classes. I would have to wait in the car until her classes was over to drive her back home. It had shifted so far from me being a member of the church or a mentee to what felt like an indentured servant. Work was the only place other than school that I felt free. It was customary for my workplace to have a staff meeting a few days before school was set to start back. I was glad to see many of my colleagues after the long summer break. We would usually have these meetings to set the focus for the upcoming school year and to meet the new staff that were to come on board.

I looked up from my documents as the meeting was set to start and that's when I saw him looking at me. He was tall slim built with his hair corn rolled to the back. He wore an oversized bright red t-shirt and jeans with red and white Nike sneakers to match. He took away his gaze after he found out I caught him looking at me. That was Corey. Corey was high energy. He was sincere in his tone. He was excited to be an educator. He was going to be taking on a challenging group of young men for the upcoming school year. I wondered how he would manage. I was thrilled that these young men would have a young black male teacher that could possibly inspire them and give them a different glimpse of the black male image. I believe that the presence of a man represents order. Especially in the lives of our black and brown boys. The absence of fathers in the home has impacted our world in so many ways. Ways that will take lifetimes to reshape. I was just as excited for Corey and these young men about what that process would look like. Corey represented a light in a dark place for those young men. He introduced himself to me. I welcomed him a board and extended myself to him and if he had any questions, I would be upstairs on the 4th floor. From the way he looked at me to the way he extended the conversation I felt he might be taking an interest in me, but I didn't give it much thought. I always had the thought of all I went through with Trent and didn't want to get back in that kind of situation again.

While the meeting was going on I became distracted for a few moments in my own thoughts. Rent, car payment and car insurance were due. I spent the summer away in Boston trying to finish my graduate degree, so I didn't have a chance to work. It was a stressful time. My focus was locked in on my plans of self-improvement.

After the meeting, I went to finish setting up my classroom. Corey came up several times asking for tape, scissors, bulletin board paper, etc. I was glad to assist him. I completed what I had to do there, headed to the hair salon to get ready for the first day of school to start the following day. Once I got home, showered and laid my new white blouse and black skirt out. I wanted to look good to meet my new students. I placed my work bag by the door and did a meal prep, I didn't want anything slowing me down in the morning. I was exhausted. I crawled into bed and set my alarm clock. I took a deep breath. As I was exhaling my phone ring. It was Apostle Ruth calling. "I've been calling you all day!" she said with disgust in her voice. "I'm sorry, I was getting my classroom together and in meetings, I was not near my phone". I explained" School starts tomorrow. I really was not near my phone. I contin-ued to explain. "Well, I just got invited to preach out at a popular church tomorrow night, I need you to write and introduction for me". Ruth said. I put the phone down. I couldn't believe her re-quest. "Hello are you listening? Ruth asked. "Yes, I'm listening. I tried to explain that I was already lying down. I had to get up early. She just continued. "I'm telling you daughter, there is a blessing in the pressing. Press your way past being tired. As you press you way to be a blessing to me God is going to bless you and give you the strength you need" she said. "Let's not forget, I allowed you to go back to school on two occasions. I got you a laptop to help you do your work. You promised me that you doing all these things would not interfere with what the Lord needed you to do. Okay get that done for me sugar and send it in enough time for me to go over it before I preach tomorrow night." She demanded. I stayed silent. As she continued to talk and go into prayer, I got up from my bed and begin to work on the sermon. I thought why me for a moment. I thought this was an act of my faithfulness. But why did it feel this way. I often wondered about the residue that lingers on a person's life that has went through abuse. Are there invincible signs attached to that person that says, "hey pick me I want to be mistreated and mishandled". Is it because that person suffers from "sociotropy"? A personality trait or feeling overly concerned with pleasing others and earning their approval as a way to maintain relationships. I always felt the strong need to nourish everyone else without adequately nourishing myself. I felt beholden to her. I was drawn by her stance she took as a woman in leadership during a time when women in leadership especially black women in leadership was not popular. Throughout the years I learned more that this behavior was misandry. There were never any good depictions of men in her view. The men that were in the congregation were docile men that served her over their own wives. I never really understood it, because the message preached was obedience is greater than sacrifice and I just wanted to be obedient to God. I wanted to be obedient to the apostle. I felt beholden to her, she had done so much for me. I had no right to say "no". I made sure I wrote the sermon and emailed it to her it was 3:04 am.

I thought about the prophecy she gave me a few years back when I first started to attend the church. God is going to send you a good husband, one that will love you. I tried hard not to think about that prophecy because I was yet to divorce Trent. Trent had been out of the picture for some time now. Family members would call me to say they saw him and how he didn't look good. I would tell them please do not call me to speak about him. I do not want to hear about him. I moved on with my life years ago. Sorry you didn't get the memo. I was one payment away from finalizing my divorce. I met a great attorney that was willing to let me make monthly payments to get it done. It was finally about to be official. Although we had not been together for years it was the legal aspect, I needed to overcome to solidify me decision. Once I made my final payment, I needed Trent to agree to sign off on the paperwork. I decided to reach out to his mom to get his phone number. We had an interesting conversation. "You know Toya, I always loved you, you were a good young woman" His mom said. "I didn't realize my son had some deep-rooted issues, he was always a sweet kid and wanted to do his best to help out around the house, but he was different than my other kids', she explained. "You know a mother will have 5 children and each child will be different. Some may have similar ways but each one will need more or less from the mother". She stated. "Trent was the one that needed more than I could give, I prayed for my son and tried to help him, I don't want you to think I raised him that way because I didn't. I thought he had outgrown those behaviors, but when I found out why you left him I knew those old childhood behaviors had resurfaced. She spoke. I just listened as she spoke. It was comforting to know that she knew the real reason behind why things didn't work out between us. "Just because you are divorcing him, doesn't mean you are divorcing me. She said. I laughed. "No never Ms. Rachel, you will always be a part of my life. I spoke. She gave me his number. I ended the call.

"Hey Trent, how are you? I asked. "I'm good, working hard you know doing what I have to do". He spoke. "Oh, that's great, you always were a hard worker. I spoke. I had to be extra nice. I really needed him to sign the divorce papers. "So did you get the papers, I sent a money order as so you can pay to get it notarized and a self-addressed envelope to make everything easy" I explained. "Yeah, I got it, I heard you teaching now. Why couldn't you do that while we were together, you know with you teaching and me working we would be doing good now. How about I rip these papers up and we work things out, I'm different now, I got saved". He spoke. I could have passed out at this point. Remain cool I told myself, you need to get these papers signed. "Well I'm glad you gave your life to the Lord. Honestly maybe things could have worked out if that was the will of God concerning us. But it was not. It's like having a flower garden. The flower in the garden have needs for them to flourish. It must have all the right components to be successful. If that flower is not nurtured, if it is trampled on, if its cut prematurely or faced extreme conditions that flower will not survive. No amount of water or nourishment can revive that flower. It must be cut down. Sometimes the seed of the flower must be placed in conducive conditions, new soil, new nurturer in order for it to achieve its purpose. I'm that flower Trent. God is my vinedresser. Allow me to grow and flourish. He stood quiet. Then replied okay I will sign it but I'm only signing it because that's what you want. He said "Yes this is what I want, I appreciate it. Be well. We ended our phone call.

I'm grateful that Trent finally came to terms with the fact that we were not going to be together again. I wanted to celebrate with someone I felt would be happy for me. So, I called Ruth and invited her to dinner to share my exciting news. While at dinner, I told Ruth I had some exciting news. "Trent agreed to sign the divorce papers" I said. "Oh really, he agreed?" Ruth said. "Yes and I am so excited, I'm finally closing that chapter of my life". I explained. She obviously could see how happy I was. I was gathering my things to get ready to leave because dinner was over a half hour ago, I intentionally waited until it was over to tell her. I had to start outthinking her if I wanted to have a moment of happiness about my accomplishments. "Oh, and I want to also share with you that I'm going to put in for a few days off from work. I want to go see my parents in South Carolina. It's been a long time since I went there to see them. The last time I saw them, they came up here and we couldn't even spend that much time together because they only came for the weekend and that weekend we were in church. I had plans to spend four days with them. I explained. Ruth remained quiet for a moment as she didn't give me a quick response, but by the time she eventually gave her response, I was surprised by what she said, "the lord is not releasing you to go see your parents." Apostle Ruth said to me. I was speechless for a moment. I missed my parents so dearly, why was God not releasing me to go see my parents? I asked" I don't know why, but right now is not the time. You must be equipped spiritually to go see them. That's the problem with folks, they always getting ahead of God and get themselves in trouble. Sint that man down there, are you trying to go lay up with him? Ruth asked after she noticed I was frowning. "No." I responded reluctantly. "Are you done with the coursework I gave you to help me out with?" Ruth asked. "What? I spoke. I was so confused. "I just told you that he agreed to sign the divorce papers, why would I go to be with him? That makes absolutely no sense! I spoke. "Watch your tone, are you trying to go up against what the Lord is saying? Ruth said. "No, I'm not, I just miss my mother and father. I miss my family. I'm always around you and these church members. I want to go around my real family". I spoke. "Well, I'm sorry to tell you that this is a lonely road and you will have to be rejected. Jesus was rejected. I was rejected. My mother never liked me, she treated my sister better than me. I never knew my father. I had to go without having much. I had to struggle. I went to school hungry; I could not learn that way. I used to steal food. I married for food. I used to be hungry all the time. I learned to go without. I'm trying to teach you the same thing because you are just like me. She spoke. The only difference is I didn't have any one to walk me through. She explained. I just listened. I knew she had gone through a lot of things, but I was not like her. I knew my family loved me. They didn't understand the nature of my relationship with her. They didn't understand why I was always around her and not them. My father would call me up on the weekend and ask what I was doing. I would say "oh you know I have to take Apostle somewhere." He would be furious. "Why are you always with her. I never seen anything like that in my life. I want grand kids; you'll never have them being under that woman. She already lived her life. I'm not the smartest man in the world but something is not right about her". My father said. "No Daddy, you don't understand, don't say that about her she has helped me a lot. I spoke. "I don't care what she did, she is a pastor, she is supposed to help people that's her line of business. But you are a young woman 25 years old, you're supposed to be enjoying your life, not living like that, you can love God and enjoy life. That church must be a cult. Yeah, that's what it is it's a religious cult. My father said.

Having all this on my mind I knew I had to go see my parents, just to show them that I was not in a cult knowingly and I could go and come as I please. "The lord has me on another assignment. I need you to write another introduction for a sermon for me. She spoke. "I can't do it" I said. "I have a lot of work to do before I am set to leave. I explained. "Well, I would like you to do it on the laptop I brought for you. You can't only do your work all the time, my work will have to be done too. If I would have known you were not going to do my work, I would not have brought it for you". Ruth said. I could remember her saying that she was giving me the laptop to help me in doing my work, but ever since she gave me the laptop, I've been doing more of her work with it than my own work. After our conversation, I went home and started working on Ruth's sermon. I always felt like if I did not do what she asked me to do, God was going to deal with me. I had issues with sleeping that night because I kept thinking about what Apostle Ruth meant when she said that God didn't release me to go see my parents. It was more like she wanted me to stay around and continue being at her beck and call. I didn't want to admit this, but a great part of me believed that this was certainly the case. I had left Trent, and I would soon be having a divorce to be completely free from him. Walking away from Trent was just like walking away from a cage; it was like walking away from some kind of prison, but I didn't leave the prison that I was confined to with Trent just to get into another prison with Ruth. I never understood why she could preach on Sunday, take you through deliverance then tell you off on Sunday night. She used to talk about how she would have her way with men, spending money, taking her on trips and buying her expensive gifts before she surrendered her life to God. Yet she did not submit her mind to the word of God. She lacked the fruit of the spirit. Ruth was gifted in her ability to persuade people, but she lacked the fruit of the spirit. This behavior was damming to many. This behavior damaged people souls that were saved. This behavior didn't consider one's love for God, it manipulated it and toyed with the psychology of believers. It was no way any of this could be right. The thought of this was beginning to bother me a lot. While I was living with my sister and her roommate, I didn't have my own space; I had to share the little space with my sister and her roommate. It was uncomfortable for me and uncomfortable for them because I was changing quickly for the better. I didn't want to be around a lot of things. Now that it was just my sister and I, I had my own room and space. Yet I felt more trapped. It felt like most of my freedom had been taken from me. How can you be free and bound at the same time? I often asked myself. I didn't know how long I had to endure this, and the problem was that it was never getting better. It was literally getting worse than it used to be. I did enjoy traveling to different prayer conferences. Being with Ruth kind of offered me that opportunity, but it was obviously beginning to look like she was mishandling me, and she was doing everything to make sure I continued staying around her. I wasn't comfortable with that now; I just hoped that things would get better because I didn't know how I was going to put up with that if it continued for a long period of time. I already called my parents and informed them that I would be showing up by next week. They sounded so excited when I told them that I would be coming to see them and that I would be spending a few days with them. She expected me to devastate them and tell them I would no longer be coming because God did not release me to go see them. My parents would never accept that, they would be sure something was going on. I have not visited home for like a year now, and just when I had told them that I would be showing up, I had to say that God had said I shouldn't come. My dad would have called Ruth himself to have words with her if I had told him.

The next morning, while I was done preparing for work, I sat on the bed and then called Ruth. I told her that I was still going to see my parents. I told her that they needed to physically see me. They haven't seen me in a year and that they wanted to see me. I told her they said they loved me. This seems to bother her because she stood silent. "Okay I have to leave for work". I spoke. She never said anything, the phone just disconnected. I didn't bother to call back.

About two days later I received the divorce papers in the mail. It was like receiving my emancipation. I called up a friend of mine and shared my good news. We decided to meet for dinner to celebrate. I knew better than to call Apostle by this time with any good news. While at dinner, I received a phone call from Trent, he told me that he was sorry for the way he had hurt me; he was only able to realize how much he had hurt me since I decided to stay away from him. He then told me that if I wanted to come back to him, he was going to do his best to become a better person, but if I wanted to go, he was letting me go. I told him that I had already made up my mind to leave. My life had been far better since I left him, there was no way I could ever deny that. I now had peace of mind and didn't need to live in fear that someone would hurt me; I didn't need to go on walking on eggshells. Never knowing what would trigger him to display different behaviors. Not to mention he had a history of claiming he was going to change and then later becoming worse than what he used to be in the past. There was no way I would be taking chances on him, and most importantly, I had to admit that I wasn't feeling the way I used to feel in the past for him. I've come to realize that everything becomes irrelevant with time. I had to question if I ever really loved him, because all I experienced was pain. I believe we can mistake pain for love. Pain can be an unpleasant emotion. Pain is constructed entirely in the brain. Your brain is literally creating what your body feels. Love is also an emotion. It is deemed as a deep affection for another person. The abuser is an inflictor of pain and not love. The abuser will say I behave this way because I love you. The abuser does not know love. The abuser's behavior yields sadness, distress and unpleasant feelings. Not love. I learned I was not in love I was in pain.

But all of that was now in the past. It even surprised me that I was feeling this way now. All those things which I was feeling for him back then were now very irrelevant.

I didn't need anything from Trent. We didn't need anything from each other; our divorce went smoothly. There were no children in between, no assets. Nothing to divide nothing to share. We both went our separate ways to live our separate lives.

chapter eight

COULD BE
LOVE

The staff meeting had been delayed for about ten minutes. So, I was seated in the conference room with a few other colleagues; we were waiting for our administrators to come in so we could commence the meeting. It was a Friday. We rarely had meetings on Friday; I didn't know why they didn't just have to wait until Monday before we would be having this meeting. I had just finished grading some papers as I was preparing to leave when I heard over the intercom " All staff please report to the conference room for and emergency meeting. I hated when they called emergency staff meeting especially on a Friday, because it rarely was an emergency. It was just someone wanting to aggravate us before the weekend. So, as we were seated and waiting for the meeting to begin. I begin to work on my lesson plan for Monday, I didn't want any of my time to be idle time. While writing my pen stop working. I then started looking for another pen. I couldn't find it. I did not want to go back upstairs to my classroom just to retrieve another one. I was so bothered by this. I needed to be working while we waited for this meeting to start. "Can I borrow your pen?" I asked the person behind me on the left. "I didn't come with any." He responded. "Can I borrow your pen?" I asked the person by my right, please?" I asked the person by my right. He quickly checked for his pen and couldn't find it. "I can't find it." He responded. Someone then dropped a pen before. He was standing behind me. I then turned to look at whom it was,it was Corey. He took me by surprise. He was just walking in. He obviously saw me asking for a pen and then volunteered to give me his. I found myself smiling at him. He smiled back at me. "Thank you," I said to him; he shrugged and then went and sat at his usual place. Yes, at this point, I can't deny that I liked this man, he was always so pleasant, but I still kept my distance, and never talked much to him; the fact that we were not teaching the same grade kind of limited the possibility of us seeing one another frequently.

Now, the meeting was over. I had forgotten for a moment that the pen I had been using in the conference room wasn't mine. By the time I remembered, I had looked around but couldn't find Corey. I quickly ran out of the conference room. He was already heading to his classroom. I didn't want to go into his class; I told myself that I had to catch up to him before he got into his class, no matter what. I met him walking in the hallway. I quickly ran and accosted him. He was surprised by the way I had ran into him.

"I'm sorry I forgot to give you your pen after the meeting. So, I had to run to you down to give it to you." I said while breathing heavily. "It's just a pen; you should have just kept it," Corey said. "No, that's not right. You didn't ask me to keep it when you gave it to me and believe me, it was very helpful to me, very helpful that it would be very disrespectful to refer to it as just a pen." I responded with a smile. Corey chuckled. He looked even more handsome when he laughed; I had to take my gaze off him immediately before he would be able to notice that I was tripping for him already through my eyes. I felt like he would be able to see things just by looking at my eyes. "If you insist, I will take the pen then." He then took the pen. I then turned to leave almost immediately. "Hey... Hmmm... I mean, what's your plans for this evening? Like, are you free for dinner tonight?" Corey asked. The question was so out of the normal, but I loved every bit of it. I then turned and looked at him. "Sorry," I said to him. I'm usually not free on a Friday night? I didn't want him to know that I was going to be in the church that night, and I was going to be speaking for the youth conference. I couldn't leave that for anything as bad as I wanted to . I felt bothered that the program I would be speaking at would kind of prevent me from grabbing this moment, but I was happy; at least he made a move. "Where will you be going tonight?" He asked. I didn't expect him to ask, but he did ask. "Church," I said with a smile. "Can I come?" He asked. I stared at him for a moment, was he being serious? He waited for my response. He wasn't joking, but he had smile on his face. "Sure, if you want to," I responded.

During the evening. The youth conference at the church was on. Corey was seated close to the front row from where he could clearly see everything that was happening on the pulpit. He came on his own; I didn't get a chance to acknowledge him at the service.

I never told Apostle Ruth he was coming, so she didn't know who he was or whatever. God used me mightily that night as I was on fire for the Lord. I spoke about Queen Esther and how she changes the heart of the king. I encouraged the young people to follow the voice of God because he has called us for such a time as this. Now, after the service was over, I knew Corey wanted us to meet, but I didn't want to meet with him at the church not just yet. So, I told a friend of mine in the church to give him a ride and then drop him at the nearest gas station. I'll be meeting him there. My friend took Corey and then dropped him where we had agreed to meet. Within just a few minutes of Corey getting there, I was there with him. He felt so delighted to see me. I was scared because a great part of me wanted him to still like me after he heard me minister the word of God. I already knew he was interested in me prior to seeing me at church, but I was not sure how he would feel after he saw me. It takes a special kind of man to support a woman in ministry. A special kind of man to cover her in prayer and not compete with her. It takes a special kind of man to be secure in who he as he pushes his lady into her purpose. I was praying Corey would be that kind of man. Corey told me how much he was impressed by the service and how good I was with what he saw me do in the church; he was filled with a lot of words of praise and encouragement. My mind became at peace because this man whom I was falling for was so delighted with the fact that I was in the house of God and working for God.

There were different churches represented at the youth conference that evening. Many young people were blessed that night and gave their life to the Lord. The visiting churches begin to request for me to speak at their church they believed the Holy Spirit was using me mightily. It was inspiring for them to see a young woman on fire for God. As for Corey, he didn't stop coming to the church. He would attend his service first and then meet me at my service just to take me out for lunch. I was reluctant to tell Apostle that I knew him and that we were seeing each other. I was fully aware of how she would respond. When other women in the church would bring a man to the service, she would start preaching about the man, she would say that the man was not the one for the woman. She would say that the man was sent by the enemy to destroy their lives. So, the man would never come back to the church. The women would continue being single and lonely. I didn't want her to do this to Corey, so I elected not to mention anything about him to her.

chapter nine

A NEW START WITH A NEW PRICE

Today was a very important day in my life; I just got my results for my state certification exam. I passed! I was so happy because I knew how difficult it was to achieve this, considering how tight my schedule was. So, Corey wanted us to have dinner together. It had been about four months since we became close. He had sometimes taken me out after work for dinner but this looked somewhat different since it was coming after I passed my exam.

While we were eating, Corey suddenly stopped eating. He then looked at me, I noticed he was looking at me, so I looked at him too. "I love you, and I have been telling you time will reveal the depths of my heart." He spoke. Honestly, it felt like the ground was going to come from under me, because everything about us feels so right. I have never been this happy in my life. I want to keep this feeling. I want to be with you. I want to breathe the air you breathe. He spoke. As he spoke, I felt every word he confessed to me down into the core of my soul. "I know your past; I know how badly you were hurt, God sent me to heal your hurt. The bible says that a man that finds a wife, finds a good thing and obtains favor with the lord. I want you to know tonight that I believe I have found my good thing and I want my favor with God" Corey said. I basked in the moment. It was a intimate moment. Two hearts and souls were connecting. I felt so secure around him. He was everything I wanted and needed in a man, and he knew exactly what he wanted, he was well educated, well-traveled, loved God, his family and knew how to save money. I then smiled at him, "I love you too, Corey." I said to him. He pressed his lips against mines. I could feel all his love in that moment.

That night, I called Ruth and then told her that I was now seeing someone. She was surprised that she couldn't talk for a moment. "Who is he?" She finally asked. I told her it was Corey. She already saw me speaking with him at the church. She just told me to be careful with him because he looked like someone that wouldn't be a good man for me. "Tell him to keep coming to the church and we will see what the Lord says about him." She spoke. I didn't respond. She said have a blessed night and I hung up the phone. That night all I could do was smile. I really couldn't think about what Ruth had said because for some reason I could hardly hear her in my head. I could only hear what Corey had said and how it made me feel. I slept throughout the night.

My relationship with Corey continued to grow deeper. I was very open about him. I was not going to keep him a secret. I was proud to be with a high value man. He was proud to be with a high valued woman. A woman rich in spirit and love. An unperfect woman. A woman who suffered from bruised love. He introduced me to his friends and family. I introduced him to my friends and family. Everyone was excited about us and a possible future with us.

One faithful evening, I had returned from a date with Corey, got home, undressed and went for shower. I felt so loved. I didn't know when I last felt this way. I don't think I ever felt this way. Corey knew how to make me feel like a woman was supposed to feel. My life just changed after I allowed him in. How could love be this sweet? Immediately I stepped into the bedroom; my phone started ringing. It was Corey. He called to say he made it home and that he loved me and missed me already. It had barely been thirty minutes since we left each other, and he was calling to speak to me. He made me feel so special. At the same time, I was having a conversation with him. I noticed that I was getting another call in. I knew that it could only be Apostle Ruth calling me, since I had my phone on silent while I was out with Corey. I ended the call with Corey and quickly answered.

"I have been calling you all evening, you must have seen I called, you didn't even bother to call me back, that's not like you" she said. "You must be entertaining another spirit that is not of God" she said. " A few months back you would call me and tell me everything, now I have to call you multiple times just to get a hold of you". Ruth said. I felt like she was complaining. But I was with her earlier during the week, and we spent a long time together. "You forgot three days ago, we were together" I said to her. "That was three days ago. Honestly, this Corey you're seeing is trying to take you away from me. He's taking your anointing away from you." Ruth complained. I knew she never liked him, or maybe she never liked the fact that I was with him. She was always feeling insecure whenever I was with him, but I had never failed in helping her do all the things which I had always helped her do. I just didn't understand why she was feeling that way about Corey. He was a very good guy; he treated me with the utmost respect, he supported me and truly loved and cared for me. How could she not love that for me? I didn't know what to say to Apostle Ruth; I just felt uncomfortable with what she was saying.

"Where is he from?" Ruth asked. She had asked me this question like five times before. "I mean, where is his family he from? And who are his parents?" Ruth asked. I was going to say something, but she quickly stepped in, "How much do you know about this man? You see the enemy sends wolves dressed in sheep clothing. Yeah, it starts off all good, but after a while you will see that wolf will rare his ugly head. " Ruth explained. She was in control of the conversation without allowing me to say much. It looked like she was laying the groundwork to tell me why he wasn't the one for me. "The members are talking about the Gucci bag you had at the service on Sunday, where did you get that from? When I met you, you aint have nothing. She spoke. "Corey gave it to me as a gift ". I said. "Well don't wear that here anymore, people will think you sleeping with him". She spoke. "I don't care what people think, they don't know what's going on and I don't care what you think, I'm a grown woman". I wanted to say so badly. But as usual I stood quiet and let her talk. I said goodnight and hung up the phone.

Ruth continued to be a big-time issue between me and Corey. I had to start hiding Corey from her. Whenever I wasn't at home, she wanted to know where I was to make sure I wasn't staying out with Corey. She announced in church the following Sunday that she had put together a "governing board". This governing board was put in place to keep watch over the members, they were assigned by Apostle to ride pass the members house to see if a man was going in or coming out. If you were to be caught you were going to be tried in front of the governing board and reprimanded.

Whenever I was with Corey, I had to ask him to keep quiet before I would respond to her call so she wouldn't find out I was with him. I believe sometimes she knew I was with him; she would call me and start praying for an extended period of time just to keep me on the phone. Corey was patient and did not interfere. Things were really getting serious; it was as if I was in prison, even a baby had more freedom than I did. I was feeling suffocated; I didn't know how long I could last. I couldn't breathe!

One Saturday morning at 5 am prayer, Ruth found a ring on my finger. She was surprised. She asked me how I got the ring, and I told her Corey had asked me to marry him, and I accepted. She was disoriented. She was clearly not happy. She felt threatened. Yeah, Corey proposed, and I accepted, and it's been about two weeks already. I couldn't tell her because I knew her stand on my relationship with Corey.

The next Sunday was not a good one. A lot happened in the church. The end was approaching quicker than I expected. I was sitting in the church. Ruth was preaching from the pulpit; she suddenly digressed from what she had been preaching. "Someone in here is trying to get married, but it's not going to work, because God is not in it. That man is going to beat her for breakfast, lunch and dinner; he's not the one meant for her. This person thinks they're going to have the wedding of the year, but she won't. It'll be a total disaster," Ruth said. While she was speaking, I felt so disgusted; I didn't know she could go this far. As she spoke, God spoke within my spirit, "exposure is coming to this house," he said. I remained seated without saying anything. While she was speaking, her slip that she wore under her skirt fell around her ankles. I took a deep breath, trying to gather my thoughts. She continued, " if they leave this church, they'll preach from a garbage can." She said while walking down the aisle, she was now screaming and yelling in a possessed manner. I've never seen her this way before. I was in total disbelief." "These demons think they can come in here and steal my sheep. Well they can't. The devil is a liar". "We have to war people of God." Ruth proclaimed. The congregants looked confused yet the followed her command and begin to speak in a strange "tongue". It was spooky. Then the clock suddenly fell off the wall, and God spoke to me, "your time is up here." It was very clear to me that day I had decided that I'd had enough. I got up from where I was seated and then left the church. It was my last day in the church. I got outside to my car and vomited. I was so sick on my stomach. What was happening? I was confused and perplexed, I could barely make it home.

I got into my house, locked the door and screamed to the highest pitch. I cried, I punched my pillow, I vomited again. "God what did you do to me?" I yelled. "I' m never going back to church! How could you let this happen to me"? I was devasted.

While in this mood of complete devastation, my phone rings, it was Ruth. "Hello, are you ready to talk? "Ruth asked. "I have nothing to say, "I said. "I'm not doing your wedding, I will not marry you two, he is an abuser, he's going to beat you . You will not blame the church". Ruth said. I listened with tears streaming down my face, my nerves were all over the place. She continued." Call your mother and father, get them on a three-way, I want to speak to them. They need to know what the lord is saying. Ruth insisted.

I joined my mother in on the call. "Hello sweetie". My mother said. My mother was unaware of what was going on. She did not know that Ruth was on the line as well. Ruth immediately interrupted. "I just want you to know your daughter is disobedient and that man is not the one. The church will not be responsible for what he will do to her, I've warned her, and she is walking in the spirit of disobedience". Ruth explained. My mother listened for a moment to what she had to say without interrupting. When Ruth paused. My mother asked, "Are you done?" Ruth responded. "Yes, the Lord has spoken!" "Well, you have said a lot, and I want you to know all of what you said is not what the Lord is saying, her father and I have accepted Corey as our soon to be son-in -law. Her grandmother, the matriarch of our family has given them her blessings. He has been kind, respectful and loving to our daughter and that is all that matters. It is fine if you do not do the wedding, she doesn't need you to do it. She will not be returning back to that cult of a church your running; the lord has set her free. My mother said. "Have a good day," said my mother. The call disconnected. As angry as I was, I felt a relief in the moment. My mother had protected me. My mother supported me as she always had. A mother's love runs deep. A mother's love is unmatched. A mother will always want what is best for her child no matter how old they are no matter how far away they go. A mother's love will always secure the heart.

A few moments a passed. Ruth was calling my phone again. I picked up but did not say anything. "Are you leaving me? Are you leaving me? Answer me!" Ruth screamed. I never heard this tone before, I did not recognize it. "Your leaving me for this no good man", "He's going to beat you, he doesn't love you!", "He will never touch your womb! What about the school, you said you would help me!, What about my doctorate degree? You owe me! People from the church wanted to come and hurt you, I stopped them! " Ruth yelled. It was unreal what was unfolding. Ruth was sobbing and shouting. Ruth wanted to break me. "Just call the wedding off, keep the ring, come to my house so we can talk". Ruth said. As she continued to plead with me. The scripture was unfolding right Infront of me. 2 Corinthians 11:**13** For such men are false apostles, deceitful workers, masquerading as apostles of Christ. **14**And no wonder, for Satan himself masquerades as an angel of light. **15**It is not surprising, then, if his servants masquerade as servants of righteousness. Their end will correspond to their actions. I took a deep breath and with every fiber of my being. I said " I am still going to marry him and I am not coming back to you or your church!. I hung the phone up. I had finally stood up to Ruth and made my position clear.

chapter ten

THE CHAIN IS BROKEN

After I left Ruth, she didn't call me for some days, but later started showing up at my workplace. She would park her car directly in front of the school that I worked at. She would be there in the morning when I arrived for work and in the afternoon as I was leaving. This went on for about two whole weeks. I maintained my cool. I didn't know she was this way. If I had known she was this way; I would have never step foot in her church. It was as if I left prison only to walk into another prison. Leaving Trent was one battle only to walk into a battle with Ruth.

No one from the church reached out to me. It was forbidden. I had seen it before, anytime someone would leave the church, she would instruct us to cut all communication with that individual. She would declare them as an enemy to the church. A demon.

"When they come up against me, they come up against God". Ruth would say.

God continued to bless me. I never lacked anything that I needed. I was growing in what I was doing. After I left Ruth, I had more time for myself than I used to in the past. I found out that all the things that had always kept my life looking very busy were things that had to do with her.

My wedding with Corey was the best I could ever ask for. We were surrounded by love. The love for us was so strong that nothing could penetrate it. We were so happy, and all the people that came around were so happy for us too. I had already cut the relationship with Ruth, she preached about me for weeks as I was told later. She told the members if they go to my wedding God would deal violently with them.

I was used by her. She abused me by gaslighting, guilt tripping and gate keeping me; I needed time to heal from all that. I never knew that some people could abuse people in the name of the lord. They would take advantage of you. She enslaved me in her fowler's snare for seven years. I believed that my faithfulness in serving her meant that I was faithful in serving God.

After I left Ruth, I contemplated never going to church again and never trusting spiritual leaders, but my husband Corey prayed for me. He knew I loved God, and I loved church. He prayed for me daily, especially on Sundays. Sundays were painful. My faith in church and ministry was gone. I was on an emotional rollercoaster.

Some days I was hurt other days I was angry. Ruth's bitter words would replay in my head.

I tried to visit other churches, but I was never truly connected the least reminder of Ruth made me hesitant about connecting to anyone. But one day I received a phone call from a close friend I consider as brother. He called to invite me to a Sunday service taking place not too far from where I was living at the time. He had been telling me about the Pastor and the church for months. "Toya "he said. "You have to come with me to this church, I'm telling you God is truly there". "This woman Eunice is anointed". He spoke.

"Woman" I said. "No thank you!", You know how I feel about women in ministry". He continued" I know, I know, but I'm telling you this is different, I know what you went through, but God allowed that to happen for a reason, God is working something out in you, God is going to use what happened to you to help someone else. You must trust him don't charge him!" I promise you, you won't regret it, and besides if you do, you can blame me". We laughed and I agreed.

I wore a pair of jeans and a long overcoat to the service. I had my hair tucked under a baseball cap. I didn't want to be noticed. Not this time around. As I walked into the church I was blown away. The edifice was beautiful. Cathedral ceilings that formed into arches, shining wooden floors, chandeliers hanging from the arches, candlelight fixtures throughout the church and a pulpit with no chairs. I had grown used to seeing pastors sitting in the pulpit on elaborate chairs as if they were gods and goddesses sitting on a throne for all to see. But this church was different. I reached over and asked Angel my friend" Where is the Pastor?", "Oh she sitting on the front row, the one with her hands raised worshiping

God," he said. "They don't sit on the pulpit here"? I inquired. "No, they don't want any of Gods glory". I was moved by that; it was a simple gesture but a powerful statement.

As I sat there and engaged in the service. I could feel the presence of God. I longed to experience his presence. I missed God. I longed to be close to him again. I just wanted to heal spiritually and emotionally. I didn't want anyone to know me, I didn't want them to know all of what I had endured. I wanted all of God in that moment. A young man was singing angelically a song by Passion featuring Crowder "He is jealous for me, Loves like a hurricane, I am a tree, bending beneath the weight of his wind and mercy, when all of a sudden, I am unaware of these affections eclipsed by his glory, and I realize just how beautiful you are, and how great your affections are for me. He loves us, oh how he loves us." I cried out to the lord that day. I didn't want that moment to end. I was getting what I needed.

I returned a few times after that Sunday and the experience remained the same. The pastors were unique individuals. A dynamic husband and wife team. The husband reminded me of Corey in a sense, he was supportive of his wife in ministry.

They really helped me through my process without ever knowing my story. I didn't want to reveal any of my truths. I prayed to God and said" God if this is where you want me to be, please give them what they need to help me grow in your love and in your grace. You know my story; you know the things that I suffered. I still believe in you and your plan for my life". As I finished this prayer and looked up, the Pastor was standing near me. She had tears in her eyes. It was as if she knew what I had been praying about. Her face was warm, it was inviting, it was sincere. She had a resonating tone in her voice. She softly said. "God loves you, he told me to tell you he's going to use you in a mighty way, everything you went through he is going to use it for his glory. I see you preaching, I see you helping women, I see you going forth without fear, without guilt and without shame. For the Lord has anointed you for such a time as this.

Horace Greeley said in a quote, ''It is impossible to enslave mentally or socially, a bible-reading people. The principles of the bible are the groundwork of human freedom.''

I found out that I couldn't remain enslaved mentally or socially. I learned that the crossover begins with the harness of character. I learned who I was through every adversity I crossed over.

I was able to find who I was through my relationship with God. I was able to discover the capacity of the human spirit to triumph. When I sat down and thought about how I lived my life while I was under the control of Ruth. I didn't know how I survived. I was conflicted mostly. I never trusted my own ambitions outside of approval from Ruth. Years later I started reading about what constituted as a religious cult. I found myself checking off all the indicators of a cult. Ruth's church was no religious community. It was a cult that opposed critical thinking, isolated members, penalized them for leaving, demanded inappropriate loyalty to her as the leader, dishonored the family unit and cross biblical principles with self-indoctrinations. My breakaway marked my freedom. Breaking away marked my first deep breath, my first exhale outside the black cult church.

It was clear that Apostle Ruth's church was twisted with fear and hatred. It blead with control and manipulation. It was seasoned with the invalidation of people and their ideas. It was all done in the name of God. But the chain of bondage was broken and I was set free.

According to Matthew 7: 21-23 "Not everyone who says to me, Lord, Lord,' will enter the kingdom of heaven, but only the one who does the will of my Father who is in heaven. Many will say to me on that day, Lord, Lord, did we not prophesy in your name and drive out demons and in your name perform many miracles? Then I will tell them plainly, I never knew you. Away from me, you evildoers!"

www.ingramcontent.com/pod-product-compliance
Lightning Source LLC
Chambersburg PA
CBHW040149160726
48006CB00014B/1680